Don't Do Stuff You Hate

By Isaac Morehouse & Mitchell Earl

Taylor —

May this book provide clarity in the things you do and new perspectives towards your life.

Believe it or not,
Time is your asset

Contents

Forward by T.K. Coleman 7

Introduction 13

What This Book Is About 15

Part I: Escape What You Hate 21

    Escape. 23

    Why Is It So Hard to Exit a Bad Situation? 24

    The Limitations of Cost-Benefit Analysis 28

    The Inability to Make Choices 30

    When to Take Action 33

    When to Stick with Something, When to Quit 35

    Emancipate Yourself 37

    Focus on What You Don't Want 40

    Don't Aim for Goals, Remove Obstacles 42

    Do What You Love, or Have It Easy? 45

    When You're Tempted to Not Be Yourself 47

    Protest Is a Poor Substitute for Living 49

    Some Lies I Believe 50

    The Renewing of the Mind 53

    How to Live Your Values 56

    The Paradox of Survival 58

    The Myth of Misanthropy 60

Question Yourself Daily...62
Why You Should Move Away from Your Hometown......65
Why Kids Do What Their Parents Do 68
Leaving Your Parents' Nest 70
Hanging Out with People Your Age is Overrated 73
A Key to Better Conversation with Anyone 75
Want to Be Interesting? Be Interested............................79
Fearing Sameness vs. Fearing Difference 81
Don't Do It to Feel Normal..83
Your Student Debt Is Unfair...85
A Degree Won't Make You Rich(er) 88
When It's Good to Be A Failure 97
You Can Afford to Fail...100
Fear of Success Is Real, Too 103
The Cure Is Not the Cause 106
Don't Rush Your Ideal Life; Rush Away from Boredom
....108

Part II: Create A Life You Love 111
Come Alive. 113
Are You Living on Purpose?...117
Live the Life You Want - It's Easier Than You Think...120
Begin with the End in Mind...124
How to Discover What You Really Want? Don't. 126
Do What Works for You 127

Doing What You Love and Being Happy Are Not
Necessarily the Same 129

Hedonism as Life Purpose 135

Joy and the Other 138

The Neutrality of Everything 140

Life as a Game 143

Age and Your Option Set 147

Your Lack of Income Can Be an Asset 149

Waging Generational Warfare Against Yourself 152

Debt Will Limit Your Options 155

Normal is Overrated 157

Gains from a Radically Different Daily Structure 159

Against Life Plans 163

Forget about Long-Term Strategic Planning 165

Obsessed with Options, Blind to Opportunities............ 168

Success as a Discipline 172

The Expedition of Our Age 174

You're Never Done Working Hard 176

Working Hard Doesn't [Have to] Mean Burnout 178

This One Skill Will Always Win 180

Be a Finisher 182

How to Trump Talent Twice 185

Laziness Can Be Fatal 187

Break Your Once and Done Mentality 188

   Skin in the Game 190
   Permission Not Necessary 194
   The Power of Perception 196
   As Long as It's Interesting, It's Good 198
Conclusion: Take Back Your Joy 201
About the Authors 205

Forward by T.K. Coleman

If you could pick any one activity, wave a magic wand, and eliminate the need to ever have to do that activity again, what would it be? Would it be washing the dishes? Changing diapers? Doing homework? Taking tests? Waking up early? Going to a job you don't like? Saying "hi" to strangers?

What would you choose to stop doing?

We've all been asked questions like "What would you do if money were no object?" or "If you only had 24-hours to live, how would you spend your time?" It's a fun and useful exercise to think deeply about what you really love, but this book takes a very different approach to the age-old quest for a flourishing life. Rather than using clichés like passion, love, and fulfillment as the jumping off point for creating a life worth living, it begins with hate.

The premise of this book is radical, yet simple; challenging yet consoling; irritating yet invigorating:

If you want to start living the life you love, you need to stop doing the things you hate.

Instead of spending more time visualizing your dreams, it's time to get brutally and unconventionally honest with yourself about why you insist on maintaining all sorts of commitments to things that you claim to hate doing. In the spirit of the Stoic maxim, the obstacle is the way, the insights contained in the following pages will show you how to use the very things you *don't* like as a compass for discovering and doing the things you *do* like.

At every stage of my life, I've chosen to do what I loved.

When I wanted to make friends, I took the risk of going out and getting to know people. When I wanted to be an actor, I moved to Hollywood, got a job at a restaurant, started performing in student films, and went to every commercial audition I could get. When I wanted to be on American Idol, I auditioned for American Idol. When I wanted to start a social media company, I teamed up with two other like-minded guys and we started a social media company. When I wanted to become a financial adviser even though I had no experience in the field, I studied my butt off, obtained four professional licenses, and became a financial adviser. When I first saw the woman who would later become my wife, I walked up to her, told her how I felt, and asked her out on a date.

Whatever I wanted to do in my life, I've gone after it. I can't say that I've succeeded at getting everything I've ever wanted, but I definitely succeeded at going after it.

Here's the most important lesson I've learned after a lifetime of following my passions:

Doing what you really want to do requires a degree of self-honesty that is far more painful than a lifestyle of just doing what you're told.

I believe this is the real reason why most people don't fill the empty spaces in their lives with more of what they love. It isn't because they're too busy. It isn't because they have lots of children. It isn't because they don't have enough money. It isn't because there's too much competition. It's because doing what you really want to do forces you to stop fooling yourself with bullshit stories about how you don't have a choice.

Years ago I heard Mike Murdock say the following: "A champion is someone who's willing to do what he hates in order to create what he loves." From that moment on, I decided to measure my love for things by how much shit I was willing to eat in order to have it. If I wasn't willing to suffer any inconveniences for something, I took that as concrete evidence that I didn't really love it all that much. If, on the other hand, I was willing to go through hell for something, I had the right to say I deeply loved it.

In my first paragraph, I mentioned how I've always gone after what I wanted in life. Still true. But in every one of those instances, I had to eat a lot of shit in order to do that. I worked jobs that I "hated." I put up with people that I "hated." I spent hours devoting myself to disciplines and routines that I "hated." But I never complained. This wasn't because I was a saint who believed complaining was somehow beneath me. I never complained because my pursuits forced me to be honest with myself about my real priorities.

I could have chosen to quit my shitty jobs. I could have chosen to stop putting up with unpleasant people. I could have chosen to stop doing uncomfortable things. But I wasn't doing all of these things I "hated" because I was some kind of victim. I was doing these things because I was determined to design a lifestyle that truly reflected my priorities. I saw my choices as an expression of my freedom, as a manifestation of personal power. Although I started out as a guy who was willing to do what he hated in order to create what I loved, I finally realized that I was doing the exact opposite: by forcing myself to think deeply about what I really wanted, I dissolved the illusion that I was actually doing things that I truly hated.

Most people spend their entire lives believing themselves to be helpless victims of lifestyles oriented around a bunch of activities they hate. It's almost a rite of passage for people to say things like "I hate my job" or "I hate doing the dishes." But just because we say a thing, it doesn't mean we've carefully analyzed what it is that we're saying.

This book will help you analyze and understand what you (and so many others) are saying when you utter statements like "I hate doing X." Moreover, it'll show you how to understand your options in a way that will make you truly free to stop doing the stuff you hate.

Be warned. It's really difficult to stop doing the things you hate. Because as with everything in life, there's a price to pay. As long as you keep doing things you hate, you get to experience the reward of having other people feel sorry for you. That's very addicting.

Being free to stop doing stuff you hate means taking ownership of your choices in a radical way. It means being real with yourself and others about what matters most. If you're willing to pay that price, a lifetime of freedom awaits you.

If you're not ready to stop doing stuff you hate, then you're really going to hate this book. So either way, I guess you should keep reading.

Introduction

I first met Isaac in the summer of 2015. Then, just like today, he possessed a contagious enthusiasm for life and an insatiable thirst for knowledge. What struck me first about Isaac was not only his intensity for living but also his interest in others. He immediately made connections by provoking life stories from any whose path he crossed.

It was his interest in my story as well as his personal challenge to me that ultimately provoked me to pursue my interests wherever those might lead. In a quick move, I unsubscribed from a conveyor belt headed toward law school, an MBA, and a life lived as another brick in someone else's wall. I have since continued to shed the burdening weight of activities and false obligations that do not add joy to my life. Hidden in the text within these pages are the countless sighs of relief and quiet exclamations of joy along my own personal journey toward eliminating things I hate.

The initial foundation of this book was primarily inspired by several years of Isaac's blog posts and talks. I have contributed sentences, paragraphs, and even entire chapters where passages spoke to my own experience. In that regard, the content of this road map to a more fulfilling life is a collection of complementary ideas between both Isaac and me.

The title of this book is a challenge, but also a relief. The challenge is to not let yourself settle for dullness and boredom and a life you don't love. The relief comes with the method we propose. "Follow your passion" is lofty, and probably too vague to know what to do with. Relax. You don't need to find your One True Purpose. We suggest simply shedding, one by one, everything that you know brings you down. Each time you do, you will begin to discover things previously unknown that make you happy. You still have to do the work and take the risk of pursuing them, but it's a load off just to realize you don't need to get busy finding a purpose or calling. Just remove the junk.

For simplicity and clarity, we chose to break the book into two sections and each chapter stands independent of the rest. The purpose of this separation is to provide a series of provocative thought experiments no matter your position in life. Whether you are already leading your ideal lifestyle or have found yourself amidst a cycle of disparaging obligations, we hope to speak to your situation and challenge you to *suck out all the marrow of life*.

Consider this book our invitation for you to pick back up your crayons and set to work on the meaningful labor of living. We hope our words may restore the color to your canvas, and ultimately embolden you to pursue a life worthy of your wildest dreams.

Happy reading.

--

Mitchell Earl
July 2016

What This Book Is About

Don't do stuff you hate.

I'm an extremist when it comes to this philosophy. I'm not bluffing. There are two reasons to not do stuff you hate.

The first is that not doing stuff you hate is an easier and more effective way to discover and do what you love than trying directly.

The second is that doing stuff you hate sucks. If you want to live a life that sucks, read no further. There's nothing here for you. If you'd like to unsuck your life a bit, read on.

When I say don't do stuff you hate, inevitably someone says something like,

"Easy for you to say. I hate doing [fill in the blank with thing you think you have to do] *but I have to."*

No you don't.

I mean it. It doesn't matter what you put in the blank. You don't have to do it.

There are extreme - and extremely rare - cases where not doing something you hate may result in great pain or even death. These cases are not relevant to your everyday life. Still, we love going to extremes in search of justifications for the belief in our own powerlessness, so let's address the extreme case head on.

Even in extreme cases you have a choice and acknowledging it is incredibly valuable. Once you reframe the situation in terms of choices you gain some power and freedom, even if just an inch. "I could choose [thing I hate] or choose death" is not an enviable choice, but it's the truth. It re-orients and clarifies your thinking.

This extreme example is a great way to highlight what's really going on in less severe cases too.

The real reason you choose to do things you hate is not because you have to. In the worst case, it's because you hate the perceived alternative even more. Now we're getting somewhere.

In the more common cases we do stuff we hate simply because we've never forced ourselves to examine what we do, why we do it, and what we might do instead.

The key is that, no matter the stakes, you can't avoid your own free-will and you needn't fear it. I told you I wasn't bluffing when I said don't do stuff you hate. You are when you say "I have to."

How to put it into practice

Implementation is hard. First ask yourself if you're doing things you hate. Make a mental (physical too if it helps) list. Pick the one you hate the most. Let's call it X.

Ask yourself if you can stop doing X immediately. If at all possible, stop doing it. It's pretty surprising how often it is possible.

If it doesn't seem possible to quit X, ask yourself why you're doing it. "Because I have to" doesn't count.

Let's say X allows you to avoid doing Y, which you hate even more. Ask yourself if there are any other ways to avoid Y. Brainstorm all possible alternatives. It's surprising how little we force ourselves to think of these. If there's a less hated way to avoid Y, switch.

If you can conceive of no possible alternative to X that you don't hate less you are left with two options:

1) Learn to hate X less.
2) Begin to create a path around X in the shortest amount of time possible.

Do both at the same time for maximum effectiveness.

One of the stranger things about this process is that it starts to work before you've even tried. The act of identifying the costs and benefits of doing X compared to other options tends to decrease your hatred of X a bit. I know people who hate the work they do to earn money but they don't hate their life or feel like a victim. They weighed the alternatives and determined doing the minimum amount of hated work necessary to gain something they loved was better than trying to find work that was less onerous. (There's more on this tradeoff in the book, but I don't want to get off track now and this intro is already longer than I'd hoped.)

It is very rare for a hated activity to make it through all the steps and reach the point where the two options presented above are truly all that's left. Ninety percent of stuff you hate can be eliminated immediately or quickly swapped for something better with a little imagination, effort, and self-honesty.

For those really tough X's that you can't shake, begin the hard work of learning to hate it less and work on an exit strategy. You'll gain a sense of empowerment and liberation. That's what you want more of. Keep at it.

Oh, and even if you've got a really tough X it doesn't mean you can't start shedding a host of smaller, less difficult hated activities in the meantime.

How to read this book

It's a collection of essays around a theme. Read it however you want. And, of course, if you hate a chapter quit it immediately and find a better one.

After this intro the rest of the book will not explicitly inform you of who's writing what. When the word "I" and similar pronouns are used it could refer to me or Mitchell. It doesn't really matter and won't affect the point being made, so just relax.

A final word

I am honored to be co-authoring this book with Mitchell Earl, a guy who takes his desires seriously and is willing to take bold, scary steps to bring them to fruition. He's living this philosophy in a way few ever do. Not only did he inspire me to put the book together, but he did most of the tough work of deciding the structure, making the final call on the content, and bringing a cohesive flow to the project. I hope it goes without saying that I did not hate writing this book with him.

--

Isaac
July 2016

Part I: Escape What You Hate

Escape

When was the last time you escaped? I mean fully escaped into a wonder-inducing, awe-inspiring landscape, or sci-fi, or song?

Humans are meant to escape. We are driven by the impulse to escape. It's what led us to multiply, fill the earth and attempt to subdue it. It's what drives us to space travel and interplanetary colonization. It's what allowed us to discover mind-altering substances and rituals. It is not the avoidance of living. This is living.

We all have a deep longing for escape. Within it exists a kind of homecoming. We all feel slightly out of place; we all possess an urge to return home, whatever that might mean. It is the drive to do this which lies at the back of all of our other impulses. It's a beautiful motivation. It is making peace with life and death. It is seeing beyond time and space.

I do not mean escape motivated by fear. That is hiding. I mean adventure motivated by the desire to escape in and of itself. Escape requires boldness, persistence, vision, and integrity. It is not cowardice. It is courage.

What are you escaping into? What are you enraptured by? Do you have the courage to follow it? Your point of origin is not your destination. Living is escaping.

Why Is It So Hard to Exit a Bad Situation?

The most common thing in the world is to hear someone complain about their job, their church, their school, or their neighborhood. It's almost a form of casual conversation. In many cases people don't actually dislike these things, they just enjoy ripping on them for fun. In many cases though, there is a deep and genuine frustration, boredom, annoyance, anger, or pain. Why don't people leave? Why not exit the situation for a better one? It turns out this is one of the most difficult things to do.

I don't think the primary difficulty in exiting a soul-sucking situation is for fear of the unknown. In many cases even the unknown would be better than the known frustration. I don't think it's primarily because society places a (too) high level of respect on loyalty. I don't think it's primarily because of the illusion that we can "change it from the inside" or play the role of reformer. I think these are rationalizations people give for why they stay. There is a more fundamental reason people stay in bad situations. Staying means you get to play the role of two cheap, easy archetypes with quick rewards: the critic and the martyr.

It's incredibly easy to be a critic. Hardly any effort is required to sit at the back of the room, arms crossed, and look indifferent while making an occasional sarcastic comment to the person next to you. Critics get friends. They get quick points and rally a small band around them in every setting. Every company has the critic and his cadre of cronies who circle around to hear his latest jab. Every church has the member who has meetings and conversations to discuss his or her concerns and troubles. Critics enjoy a weak form of respect and they are never alone. Even in a happy crowd, as soon as one critic peels off and stands apart, too good for the activity, he attracts others who don't want to be duped or fooled.

Being too cool is easy. Actually making good on your critiques and leaving that which you claim to be above is hard. The role of critic is not a bad one, but it's dangerous. It's dangerous because it's so easy. The way caffeine is easier than getting more sleep. Both have valuable and enjoyable uses in the short run or in certain situations as a kind of jolt into reality. But in both cases the long-run effect is incredibly deleterious to your health. If you only ever play the role of the critic you lose the capacity to exit or create. You are no longer the one in control of your life. You are a victim of and a slave to that which you critique. You need it because without it you have nothing.

It's a little harder to be a martyr, but not much. To play the martyr is to stay in a painful situation, which may sound hard but is much easier than doing things you love. Unpleasant things naturally find their way to you upon waking in the morning. Most disciplines are unpleasant at the outset. Most jobs are. Most new people are a lot of work to befriend at first. The easy route is to give just enough of an effort to stay in a situation, but never fully engage and never simply exit. Complaining about your boss or professor and how mind-numbing your day was is an easy way to get the attention of others. If the critic gets cheap popularity, the martyr gets cheap sympathy. Everyone feels bad for the sufferer. When you feed off of that sympathy and choose it over the much more challenging work of finding situations that don't make you suffer, you seek the same caffeine-like quick fix as the critic, and with equal danger.

I'll use an example I'm very familiar with. I've met many young people who hate college. They're bored, the classes are useless, the tuition is costly, the experience as a whole makes them feel dull and depressed if not openly angry. Calculated as a purely economic decision it makes no sense for them to stay. Four years, tens of thousands of dollars, and a very weak network and set of skills and knowledge gained at the end. They can think of myriad ways to get more with less. But that's not the only cost. To exit means to quit playing the role of critic and martyr. Those come with a lot of easy points.

Worse still, once you exit you forgo the chance to play those roles again. When you complain about your job or rip on your boss you won't get laughs or sympathy. You'll get condemnation. "Well it's your own fault. I told you not to drop out of school!" It's the same with churches, cities, and any other situation you can exit. Exit means giving up the cheap benefits of the critic and the martyr and adding the cost of social approbation.

It's easy to see why so many people stay in crappy situations they clearly hate. It's easier. No one gets mad at you for staying. You get cheap popularity and/or sympathy. You are not accountable for your feelings. It's always the fault of the bad situation you're in. This is one of the most tragic traps a human can trip.

The power of exit is at the core of human freedom. It is the first step on the road to genuine fulfillment and self-actualization. Once you embrace it – and the only way to embrace it is to exercise it – you begin to find, paradoxically, that it needn't be used as often as you thought. Sometimes just knowing that you are in a situation by choice and could leave at any time is enough to re-orient your outlook to a more productive, positive one.

If you want to live a great life you have to create it. Creating is learned. It's not free. To become a creator you have to first let go of the critic and the martyr. Yes, critique can be the eye-opener that leads to exit and creativity. Yes, martyrdom can bring the pain that leads to the same. It's not that you'll never play those roles, it's just that you can't live in them.

If you want to create a good life you have to first exit the bad one. Exit alone is not sufficient. Indeed some people get addicted to exit much the same way they can to playing critic or martyr. Always leaving what's not working but never building what will. Still, exit is indispensable and far more powerful than attempts at reforming bad situations. Reform is fundamentally submissive and reactive while exit is empowering and leads to the creative and proactive.

The martyr, the critic, and the coward belong together. Leave them behind.

The Limitations of Cost-Benefit Analysis

It's easy to assume a simple cost-benefit analysis is always in order for every important decision. I've found that the more important and radical the decision, the less valuable c-b analysis is. It's often little more than a way to complicate things, stall a decision, add stress, and provide cover for a choice your gut tells you is wrong but you fear to pick otherwise.

When I think about all the biggest decisions in my life they all had a moment of crisis where c-b ceased to bring any clarity. I was forced to answer one simple question – the only question that really matters – do I want to do this or don't I?

Whether considering marriage, moving to a new city, having a child, starting a business, or any other major life-altering action, c-b analysis is probably distracting you from being honest about what you want and just doing it. It's possible analyzing the pros and cons can help you discover what you really want. It's far more likely you know with your knower already, but what you want is scary or unconventional or hard to explain or justify to others, so you look for additional ammunition or an out. Push all the clutter aside. Throw away your two-columned pros and cons list. Sit down with yourself in the quiet and ask, "Do I want to do this or don't I?" Sit in it. Imagine what choosing no feels like. Imagine what choosing yes feels like. Which do you know deep down you want?

Once you honestly know the one-word answer to "Do I want this?", commit. Resolve to do it. Take some action that holds you accountable to your commitment. (Tell someone in private, make it public, etc.) The rest will follow.

Cost-benefit analysis is great for decisions that don't affect the core of your being and that have a lot of small differences worth exploring–like picking a web-hosting service or a tagline. It's woefully insufficient and even counter-productive for deciding which bold steps to take on your life journey. None of the pros or cons can really be known with any degree of certainty, and all the best decisions have more unknowns than knowns, thus fewer items that can fruitfully be put on the ledger.

Ditch the analysis. What's your gut telling you? Trust it. If you want something, go get it. There is no such thing as the perfect choice, or the right choice. There is only what you want to take a chance on and what you don't.

The Inability to Make Choices

For most of us, the first 25 years or so of life involve almost no important choices. Rather, all the important choices (and many unimportant ones) are made by someone else on our behalf. When you sleep and eat and study and what you learn and how and when you're done and why are all prescribed for you. Sometimes you get to pick one school from another, or a few classes instead of others almost identical, but for the most part, how you spend your time and energy and when and on what is laid out for you. Your job is to ride the conveyor belt.

In contrast, we all want meaningful lives. Meaning must be created, and creativity requires choices. Especially choices about what not to do, what to avoid, what to ignore, what to exclude. Many people find these choices the toughest to make. It terrifies them.

After a few work trips where my son was unhappy with the book or trinket I brought back for him, I decided to ask him ahead of time what he wanted me to get. He was a bit irritated and said he didn't care, I should just pick. He's a bit of a natural pessimist and doesn't mind feather-ruffling and cynicism. I pressed and he insisted I just pick. I did, and again he complained about it. I asked why he didn't just tell me ahead of time and he admitted that he didn't want to choose something only to regret it, because if it was his choice he'd forgo his right to complain about it.

I think that approach is more common than we might assume. If you've ever tried writing consistently you discover pretty quickly that the most difficult decisions are about what to leave out. Take this post for instance. There is so much more to be said on this topic, and so much more I believe than I can reasonably include in a single post. I've got to exclude stuff. Yet I know every caveat or footnote I leave out allows room for readers to say I missed something or got it wrong. When you create you've got to pick what's most important and leave aside many other valuable things. It's vulnerable. What if people blame you for leaving them out? They will. But if you attempt to include everything you'll never create anything.

It's amazing the number of people who have agreed with my reasons for why you should blog every day. They agree it would make them better at achieving their goals. I challenge them to try it for 30 days. Almost no one does. I'm not trying to shame anyone or claim superiority (I ignored the same challenge and tried and failed at it a few times before I really got going). The reason it's so hard is because every day sitting in front of a blank blog-editor you are faced with choices. What to write about? More accurately, what not to write about? What if I write this and it's misunderstood? But to make it understood would be way too involved. I'm overwhelmed. I don't have anything to say after all. Maybe after I'm an expert.

The thing is, the more expertise you gain the harder it is to make these choices. For every additional bit of knowledge you have it's that much more you've got to leave out when you create. There will never be a time when you're ready or when it's easy. Just start. The only way to overcome choice paralysis is to make choices. Start with small, easy ones to train yourself in the fine art of creativity by exclusion.

Most of us have a lot of bad habits and mindsets we need to unlearn in order to create meaningful lives. First among them is the ability to make choices. The best part is no one is paying attention as much as you think, so you don't need to take the prospect of imperfection so seriously. Just try it. Anything that's not wrong is right.

When to Take Action

I'm highly action biased. I get the frustration of identifying a problem or having a new idea and wanting to do something about it, good and hard. I believe jumping in with both feet as soon as possible to be always preferable to lots of analysis. Still, there are times when the best thing to do is nothing.

This is particularly true when the problem is a grand one that affects all of society. Just because you realize something is wrong with X system or process doesn't mean there is an obvious and immediate action to take. The realization is the first, often most powerful but also most fleeting step. It's easy for action-biased people to get antsy and want to do something quick. Start a campaign, write an article, launch an organization, etc. Often though there is no clear vision, understanding of causal factors involved, or strategy.

Our culture is one that provides social rewards for any kind of action. If you say you're doing something to alleviate poverty, people congratulate you no matter how stupid or useless or even counter-productive your efforts might be. Volunteering is deemed noble and effective, whether or not it's either of these things. Obsession with nonprofits and vilification of win-win for profit activities further incentivizes blind action. Start a club. Host a fundraiser. Do something!

The most profound improvements in the world are typically born out of many years of following the initial identification of a problem deep down the rabbit hole. Those who see something they don't like and jump to do something come and go, as do the effects of their efforts. Those who internalize the problem – let it steep, let it alter the way they think, pursue an in-depth understanding of the problem and knowledge of tried and untried solutions, and only act when the idea they hold is one that doesn't just suggest but demands action – are typically the ones who best solve it.

There are a lot of dysfunctional beliefs and institutions around us. Discover them. But when it comes to action if you feel the itch ask yourself exactly what kind of action you want to take and why. Do your ideas demand action? That specific action? Will you be unable to sleep without taking that specific action? More importantly (and much harder) ask if the solution you have in mind can be obtained within the context of a for-profit business model. If not, the odds it will work are incredibly low.

Real solutions create value. Non-profits can create value, but it's much, much harder to know if they can and far too easy for them to do the opposite. If the solution is political it's almost assuredly going to do more harm than good. If the goal is good feels, launch a nonprofit effort or lobby politicians. If the goal is effectiveness, try as hard as you can to discover a way in which your ideas can generate a profit.

Until action is clear and value-creating, let your ideas direct you to further understanding. Channel your hunger to act towards the act of learning more. When the time is right and the idea is ripe you'll know.

When to Stick with Something, When to Quit

If you love something you don't need any reasons for doing it. If you hate something you'd better have damn good reasons for doing it.

This is about the burden of proof. If you're doing what you love and what makes you come alive, you don't need any justifications or elaborate arguments or cost.

Sure, you might find something you love even more if you keep an open mind, but you're more likely to find that by diving headlong into what's working without looking back.

If, on the other hand, you're dull, listless, feeling a bit dead inside, you'd better start asking why you haven't quit what you're doing. You'd better discover good reasons and fast.

Don't do stuff you hate.

The only exception is when something you hate meets two conditions: 1) You know it will get you to something you love, and 2) You know there is no other, better way to get there. I hated running but wanted to be someone who'd run a marathon. The training sucked, but it met both criteria. I knew it would make me able to finish the race and I knew there was no other, better way.

It's rare for something you hate to meet both of these criteria. It takes a lot of self-knowledge and self-honesty to really discover if it does. It's much easier to just keep doing stuff that doesn't make you come alive because you don't want to risk the worry or disapproval of others. But that's not any kind of life to live.

So, if you're loving something don't feel pressure to prove or explain yourself to the world. Stay alive! But if you're bored and unhappy with something, you'd better start asking questions quickly. If you can't definitively prove it will get you someplace you know you want to go and that nothing else would, stop right now. Quit as soon as possible. Exit. Keep exiting until you're not doing stuff you hate.

There's no virtue in hope if it's an aimless, indefinite hope that continuing with a job, school, relationship, or life you hate will somehow magically result in something you don't. It won't.

Knowing who we are is hard. Give yourself a break!

Emancipate Yourself

A great many people are lifestyle slaves. You keep doing work you hate because you have to to pay for a car you think is necessary because the neighbors in the place you chose to live would be leery of someone driving a beater. And so it goes, on and on.

If you really love these things and gain value over and above the suffering you endure to obtain them, fine. If not, then you have a choice to make. If you hate paying for the car and cable bill, quit. Build a new lifestyle in a cheaper house or city. Create a new standard that doesn't appeal to those around you but only the things you really value.

There is no worthy justification for living as a slave to a lifestyle you don't enjoy while you possess the ability to change it. Often it's easy to confuse desire with willingness. Wanting a better life for yourself won't make it so. You'll have to work at it. It will take time and investigation.

The number of things you do that you hate – whether going to a soul-sucking job or attending a boring social event or family reunion – is likely higher than you suspect. If you choose to examine your life you'll realize you spend tons of time and inordinate mental energy on things that make you unhappy. Many of these you can shed right now with minimal consequences. Others require planning and an escape process.

What's really holding you back?

If you admit that it's possible to do fewer things you hate, you will become vulnerable. It will shift the burden on to you to make it happen. If you embrace this philosophy the pressure is on to implement it. What if you fail? What if you say you want to quit doing what you hate to pursue something else, but doesn't work out? Better play it safe and not try.

Fear of failure and embarrassment is the major roadblock. You will fail. So what? Learn to come to terms with failure; it's a process of experimentation.

It's comfy and has some rewards to be a martyr or a critic, but it's also dangerous. The other truth is that doing things you hate or merely tolerate is easier than doing things you love. You might imagine doing what you love is easy–a lucky life for the fortunate. It's not. It's a shitton of work. Sometimes you won't quit because you won't want to work that hard.

This is not to say you need to do work you love. It all depends on what work means to you and what your other values are. Doing work you love and being happy are not necessarily the same thing. It does mean you need a great deal of self-knowledge and self-honesty to honor your values and find the courage to move ever closer to living them.

It's not just about work.

Don't limit your notion of things you hate to work. You probably have habits and relationships and other things you hate. Quit those too.

There are a million reasons to laugh at the advice. I doubt any of them will improve your life after the short-lived glow of the clever dismissal.

Things can always suck less. See if you can figure out how.

eliminate who you are NOT first

Focus on What You Don't Want

It's really stressful to feel the need to pick *the* career, job, or ideal lifestyle, and plot a path to it. How are you supposed to know yourself so well in the present, and so much about what's out there? Let alone predict what your future self will want in a future world with unlimited, unknown possibilities…

Relax. With rare exception, it's an unhealthy idea to try to pick one specific thing and try to get there. It's like shopping for the suit you'll be buried in someday. You'd be better off making a list of general categories or qualities of activities you enjoy, are good at, and/or see as valuable to get you to some other end. Still, that can be daunting.

Here's an easier approach: *focus on what you don't like and avoid it.*

Make a list of all the things you simple can't stand, are bad at, or see little value in. Anything not on that list is fair game for experimentation. Go out and earn broad experience with the explicit goal of discovering more stuff you don't like. Add it to your list. As it grows, the arena of what's fair game will narrow. Any step within that range is a step in the right direction. Each step will help clarify and reduce the possible next steps. You'll likely never have it so narrowed that only one good next step remains, but that's a good thing.

As both you and the world change, the possibilities are untold. Don't sweat finding that *one thing* right now. Figure out where you're *not* in the zone. The sooner you ditch panhandling for fool's gold, the faster you can start mining in places likely to have a mother lode.

Don't Aim for Goals, Remove Obstacles

If you're unhappy where you are, envisioning where you want to be instead might be a little too difficult. Sometimes you know enough to know you're unhappy, but not enough to know exactly what would improve things.

This makes goal-setting difficult. If a clear goal is the key to achieving it, it creates an unnecessary amount of pressure on you to have one. But there's another way to improve your situation.

There is nothing wrong with clear goals. They can be great if you can have them and be honest about them. But it's possible to make progress even with really fuzzy goals. What you want doesn't need to be clear, but what you don't want does.

Maybe you're in a job you hate. You want out, but out to what? You [think you] need X amount of income, and it's not obvious where you'd get it in a better way. It's helpful to envision whatever vague idea you can conjure of what you really want, taking into account all the actual costs and tradeoffs. Sometimes it won't be so simple to provide a clear plan of action. When it's not, go the opposite direction, instead.

Identify the things you really hate about your current situation one by one. List them out. Once you've identified the known obstacles to a better life, you can determine what action to take. Even if other unknown obstacles crop up later, you'll already have a road map to a better state.

With your list in hand, ask yourself if you can simply stop doing those things. You might be surprised to find several things making you unhappy that you can stop doing right now. If you can't, ask what is keeping you from cutting those things out. Decide what it would take to avoid ever doing those things again.

Now you have your goals.

If one of the things making your life suck is a coworker in the next office over who is profoundly rude and negative all day and you realize the only way to escape it is to quit, move to a new department, work from home, or request a different office, you now have options. You can weigh the costs of each and decide which course you want to take. Maybe you decide moving to a new department is the best way out. But you don't have the skills required.

Perfect! Now you have a clear, tangible obstacle to overcome.

Build yourself a set of daily challenges and activities to work towards gaining the necessary skills. Don't stress about the long term, ten-years-from-now-you and how these skills may or may not help you reach some fuzzy utopia. You need the skills now to overcome a real, present pain in the ass.

You'll probably never figure out the perfect mix of skills to help you get to the lofty Neverland of the distant future. But if you can identify real pain points in the here and now, you can build your self-improvement project around chipping away at them.

Work backwards from where you want to be. Identify the things keeping you from happiness. Then identify the things you'd need to do to work around, over, or through those obstacles. Then build a daily, weekly, or even monthly schedule targeted squarely at beating them, one at a time.

The stoics say "*The obstacle is the way*". For those of us without a really clear end goal, this is phenomenal advice.

Removing impediments to happiness can be a better form of goal setting than attempting to reach perfection. Your life is often more like a sculpture than a painting. Subtraction sometimes yields a better end product than addition.

Stop aiming for goals. Start clearing the path ahead of you, instead.

Do What You Love, or Have It Easy?

The hardest thing to do is what you love.

It's a long, difficult process discovering what you love; what truly makes you come alive. It includes a series of epiphanies about your own errors of judgment and direction. It demands brutal self-honesty. It requires tedious and dangerous trial and error. It cannot be found by mere reflection, but deep reflection alongside experimentation. None of this is easy, and you are never done. You change, and what makes you come alive changes. The journey toward it is endless and adaptations of your goals continuous.

That's just to discover what you love. Once you've begun to remove the chaff and to hone in on a direction that makes you fulfilled, actually moving in it is more difficult yet. You have to muster the grit and determination to move toward it, even when individual steps themselves are grueling. You must continually remind yourself what really awakens your love of life, and not let yourself off the hook pursuing anything less.

It's much easier to find and do what you mildly enjoy, what you can tolerate, or even what you hate. Anyone can stop the discovery process short and find what feels comfortable in the short term. Anyone can choose not to chisel away the distractions; not to get to the core of what makes them fulfilled. Anyone can treat what they love as an unattainable object existing only to torment and tease. Anyone can come up with mediocre, safe, reasonable, sound, and predictable goals and activities.

People say when you do what you love you never work a day. It's easy to hear that and to envy those whose profession seems to be something they have a lot of fun with. It is true that when you're in the zone pursuing your passion, it doesn't feel like work. But discovering your zone, and making yourself enter in is more work than anything.

Some people think work is hard because they're not doing what they love. In reality, they haven't been able to do what they love because they're not willing to work hard enough. Discovering and rediscovering what you love, and moving toward it every day, is the most difficult thing to do in the world. But it is also the most worthwhile.

When You're Tempted to Not Be Yourself

"Today I will live free."

These words provide me an immediate release when I write them out. I write them out when I'm tempted to focus on those things beyond my control. I write them out when I need them, when I feel the pressing weight of the Other upon me.

The Other is anything and everything that does not come from within. It's all the great ideas, people, tasks and activities bombarding me from without. They're all wonderful things, and nothing but expressions of the agency of others. Yet they're not me, and if I internalize or interact with them in any way that has a responsive orientation, I become trapped.

There is so much information out there. If my life is only to collect it, gather it, sort it, label it, react and respond to it, then I am nothing more than an automaton. But I'm not an automaton. I live and breathe passionate freedom. I can't afford to play my life in response mode. I must commit to myself and to the world that I will live free today.

Just one day. Anyone can do that, right?

So today I won't care about anyone else's information. I won't care about opinions. I won't care about any '*shoulds*' or '*oughts*' flying my way. I will care about living my journey for truth, freely and with abandon. Only then will I harness the excess creative capacity to engage fully the wide world of the Other. Only then will I live free.

Give it a try. Live free today.

Protest Is a Poor Substitute for Living

You don't have to be against something to be for something else. You can like what you like without feeling oppressed by the fact that others do not share your preferences and proclivities.

When you express the need to combat those who don't agree, you reveal a desire to gain their acceptance and a lack of self-acceptance. In so doing, you enslave yourself to their opinions, preferences, and ideas. You grant them power over your joy.

You'll never enjoy what you care about as much if you keep caring that others don't. You don't need the approval of others to live your life in a way that pleases you.

Your happiness can be independent of their permission.

Stop protesting. Start living.

Some Lies I Believe

I think Michael Jordan's Hall of Fame Induction speech where he calls out everyone he thinks disrespected him is one of the greatest lies ever. I find Alec Baldwin's "Always be closing" monologue in Glengarry Glen Ross incredibly inspirational. I loved when Kevin Durant said, "It's my fault" after playing an amazing playoff game while his teammates let him down.

Strictly speaking, all of these are lies. Jordan's high school coach didn't disrespect him. He saw an undeveloped talent and made a reasonable decision with no malice. All the employees Baldwin yelled at were not losers who shouldn't even think about drinking coffee until they can close a deal. Durant was not to blame for the loss.

Jordan chose to interpret everything as a slight. He used it as a chip on his shoulder; probably not a very psychologically healthy move in normal life. Baldwin's speech is a terrible way to manage people in the workplace. Durant's claim that he was to blame reveals a God complex that is a pretty dangerous outlook. Yet I love each of these instances.

Only once you know no one is out to get you can you benefit from pretending they are. Humans adopt beliefs and take actions based on stories. We need narratives. Sometimes, especially if you've achieved some modicum of success, life simply does not present much conflict or direct opposition.

Yet we are moved by stories of heroes and villains. This is when the truly great ones fabricate a narrative that empowers them to achieve.

When life doesn't provide those, tell yourself stories of struggle. Create myths where villains and haters are obstructing your way or mocking your effort. Don't actually make enemies with real people, but weave a narrative that produces a chip on your shoulder. Enter into a game where no one really believes in you and metaphorical bullets fly from every side.

A belief that the universe is trying to destroy you is incredibly disempowering. But once you know it's not true, yet selectively choose to play as if it is, you become unstoppable. You can't be unstoppable if nothing is trying to stop you.

So choose to become invincible if this is what you must do.

This tool will be incredibly advantageous in your arsenal. But don't use it simply to aid in the attainment of things you desire from life. Try it out in opposite circumstances. Use it to escape unfavorable situations too.

When you find yourself trapped between Scylla and Charybdis, for instance, don't pretend everyone is out to get you. Write the opposite draft instead. In this script, cloak yourself in the mentality that your present affairs are a necessary crucible you must undergo in your personal evolution.

Personify all the undesirable elements plaguing you as demons to be exercised. Then envision yourself emerging from the other side of this warfare. A survivor. A hero. A champion.

You might not be those things now, but believing is the first step to becoming. If you take up the belief that you will prevail then you already have decreased the cost of your own success. You've created a self-fulfilling prophecy which will be powerful in your escape. You're no longer running away. You're fighting through the front lines for your freedom.

The reason this mental model can be so powerful is that it emphasizes positive action in your life as opposed to negative action. It puts you back in the driver's seat. Your life no longer relies on the circumstances of others or how they intercept you. Instead, everyone becomes a player in your game.

When you do this, you'll find you no longer have to tiptoe through life on the defensive. You can live offensively. You can live boldly. You can live however you choose to. After all, when you're crafting the story, it's you alone who decides which chapters to write and which ones to avoid. Be the author in your story. Tell it however you need to.

The Renewing of the Mind

The transition from one deeply held belief to another is not a matter of intellectual argument. It's not a matter of adapting a new set of ideas on an issue; it's a matter of becoming a new person. The more deeply held the belief, the truer this is and the more laborious the transition.

It does require logical arguments. But walking through the reasons a belief you hold is false, and why an alternative is true, will not be sufficient to change your point of view for good, even if you accept the argument. You've got to go out into the world and experience things, at which point your old beliefs will creep back in, since they are comfortable and second nature. Even if you know they're wrong, you won't be able to recall exactly why. A single convincing argument is not enough to overcome years of justifications and deeply etched neural pathways. You must return to the logic, time and again and from new, surprising angles, until the conclusions no longer require work, but flow from you. You don't accept a new idea. You become a new person, one who holds that new idea.

You have to be baptized over and over until all the residue of the former belief washes off. You have to remove the scales from your eyes, layer by layer, until you see the world anew. And truly, you will see a whole new world. It's stunning how the acceptance of a different set of logical conclusions is not merely a swapping of bits of data in the brain, but a fundamental shift in the lenses through which the entire world observed. All will look different from the vantage point of the new belief.

One of the surprising things is how incapable you are after your transformation of acting like your old self. It will become impossible to even remember how and why you used to believe what you did. You may lose patience with others who believe what you once did. It would seem, coming as you did from the same place, that you'd have a keen understanding of their position. Instead, as time passes and your new self becomes more familiar, you will look at the same picture and see things so differently that dialogue becomes difficult. At this point, you must remind yourself that they, too, are on a journey, and a single conversation will not suffice to transform their mindset. You can't get them to see what you see with one dose of data. They've got to be curious enough to examine and reexamine the issue, each time removing another layer of the lens, just like you once did.

You can become many different people over the course of one lifetime. I recall some of the biases and beliefs of my former selves, and I can only smile in wonderment. *How did I persist in believing those things for so long? How much happier am I now with new eyes!* I imagine I'll eventually think the same about some of my current beliefs.

Occasionally, you might find yourself in between sets of beliefs; in a confusing purgatory of a formerly renounced belief and the full embrace of a new one. You might find yourself in situations where you no longer believe your default response, but your transformation hasn't taken full enough effect to understand your new ideas in practice. You will need to return to logic, to analyze the arguments, again and again, until your mind embodies the shift.

First, the idea will click intellectually. With enough work, you will grasp it on a gut level. Finally, when the transition is complete, you understand it well enough to explain it to others.

Arguing for an idea you haven't yet become is difficult and counter-productive, unless you're doing it as a lighthearted intellectual exercise. Become a new person, and your very life will be an argument for your beliefs.

How to Live Your Values

There is power in aligning your values with the incentives you face, and danger in having them out of sync.

It's easy to overestimate our own willpower and ability to do the right thing when the wrong thing is rewarded. An excellent strategy for staying true to your values is to assume you have zero willpower and stay out of systems that incentivize you to violate your values. The Proverbs recommend taking the long way home over walking the path that goes by the house of the "wayward woman" because you shouldn't trust your ability to resist temptation.

One of the easiest ways is to consider institutions or laws that violate your values. Then try to avoid all situations where you benefit from them. It's not always easy or possible. For instance, I may dislike government provision of roads, yet their near monopoly in this realm makes it hard for me to not benefit from and use a new road. It is, however, often more doable than we assume.

Wherever it is, try to put yourself in a position where your values align with your incentives. Don't get a job at an agency you think shouldn't exist. Don't take a contract that incentivizes overcharging or dragging out a project if you value thrift, honesty, and work ethic.

If stealing violates your core values, try not to put yourself in a position where you are desperately hungry and sitting next to someone else's unattended apple cart for hours on end.

No one is so strong that they can resists incentives to violate values indefinitely. Don't knowingly set yourself up to fail. Align your values with the incentives around you, instead.

Don't spend time with anything that antagonizes your character.

The Paradox of Survival

People who live the fullest lives have a loose grip on everything. They don't cling too tightly to relationships, possessions, health or life itself. They are free from mood-controlling fear and worry. They take the prospect of terminal illness or the loss of a job with ease, because they don't find their solace in their present material position relative to others. They invest in something deeper and more unshakable.

The ability to let go of things is useful in every arena of life. Let go of your kids rather than lamenting their choice of hobbies, or the fact that they grow and change. Let go of your fear of losing. Put yourself into your sport with abandon. Let go of the desperation to be loved or else you are likely to scare others away. Let go of fear of death, and what life you have will be all the richer.

In spite of the freedom found in letting go, humans are programmed to seek their own survival–above all else and against all odds. Are we to fight our own hardwiring? Why are humans so universally inspired by stories of fighting cancer, fighting the odds, resisting the inertia of the world, not giving up, or not letting go? We find something noble and heroic in refusal to roll with the punches.

How can we square these competing approaches? If suffering from serious sickness, is it best to let go of our fear of pain and death and find our zen? Or should we fight the degradation of our bodies with every fiber?

I say both.

There is a way to reconcile a loose grip on life with a refusal to let go of our dreams. I haven't mastered it. Few have. The space between freedom from worry and an intense focus on how to overcome it is where greatness emerges.

Consider sports. Think about Michael Jordan playfully taunting his opponent at the free throw line. Free from the worry of missing the shot or of embarrassment, Jordan closed his eyes while shooting – he maintained a loose grip on the game. At the same time, he focused intensely on dominating the game, being the best, and making the shot. Witness greatness.

The key is to hold on to what we have and keep climbing obstacles that impede us on the way to what we want. The key is also to let go of what we have and free ourselves from fear of not obtaining what we want. Now all you have to do is both at the same time.

The Myth of Misanthropy

It's normal to hate people. Everyone hates people. Fortunately, there is no such thing as people. There are only individual persons.

There are no classes, groups, nations, or any other collective capable of acting or believing. Only individuals love, hate, lie, steal, give, create, think, and act.

Collectivism is a convention of language, but it is probably the most dangerous paradigm in human history. Not only because it has led to massive violence in the hands of mobs and states, but also because of what it does to the individual. It lets us get sloppy in our thinking, and it lets us off the hook.

We like to collectivize because it lets us avoid responsibility and accountability. I can say I hate people and that people are guilty of all manner of crimes and deserve what's coming to them. But if I'm forced to point out a single, actual individual that I hate and believe ought get it, things get very uncomfortable. I want to condemn a fictitious entity and reap the self-righteous satisfaction of setting myself above it without any sort of repercussion. This is intellectually lazy, at best.

If you find yourself angry at humanity, dig a little deeper. It's often not the millions of individual actors pursuing their own ends that cause annoyance so much as certain phenomena and patterns that result from these interactions. Those are the result of the norms, rules, institutions, and incentives faced by the actors, and those can often be altered or worked-around.

It's not people that cause traffic jams or bad movies, but individual actors responding to incentives and seeking satisfaction. Maybe you can change the incentives. Maybe you can introduce new ones.

Deconstructing the collective won't necessarily make you any happier, but it can refocus your discomfort on real entities that are changeable or avoidable.

Question Yourself Daily

1. Do I like what I'm doing?
2. Is it getting me somewhere I want to go?
3. What am I giving up to be here?

These might seem like simple questions. Obvious even. Perhaps even unnecessary.

Yet so much of what we do is the result of habit, social norms, envy, fear, outside pressure, or laziness in thought and action. We often follow paths already worn whether or not they're a good fit for us. The first step in the process of waking up to a full and free life is asking these simple questions.

It's more difficult than you think, and it will take more time to answer than you think.

That's OK. Take your time. Wrestle with the questions. Don't lie to yourself. Don't ask them with a preconceived idea of what kind of person answers this way or that. If you do, you're likely to give dishonest answers – answers that reflect the person you think others might wish you to be rather than the person you actually are.

Even if everyone in the world envies what you're doing and thinks it's the pinnacle of success, fun, or fulfillment, if you don't like it, be honest with yourself. So many people stay in terrible situations simply because they feel guilty about not liking something others would love. You're not them. And there's nothing noble about suffering through something you hate unless you are firmly committed to it as a clear and definite route to something you love in relatively short order.

If you don't know where you want to go it's especially bad to suffer through things you don't like. You're suffering for no particular reason with no known payoff. It's OK to not know where you want to go. If you don't, start exploring things until you get a better idea. The fastest way to find out where you want to go is to try things and eliminate the ones you really dislike.

Finally, even if you have an idea where you want to go and you're doing something you dislike right now to get there, you need to compare to the alternatives. Just because an elaborate and expensive exotic diet and mountainside yoga routine could help you lose 10 pounds, could you have lost the same weight doing something cheaper and less painful like portion control and a little cardio?

The danger of having someplace you want to go – a goal – is that it can blind you to opportunity cost. If you know you want to reach X, and you know Y is one way to do it, you may overlook the fact that X is a lot more painful than other available alternatives, even alternatives that could lead to X and provide a lot more along the way. Just because you have a goal doesn't mean the common path to reach it is the only or best one.

Ask yourself these questions a lot. Don't panic. Don't walk out on your boss in the middle of work because you got bored for a few minutes. This isn't about being flaky or avoiding difficulty. It's about being resolute and facing adversity head on with a firm conviction about why you're doing it.

It's not about the path of least resistance. It's about having a reason – your reason – for fighting. It's about choosing your own challenges instead of floating downstream just because.

You might be amazed how many things you're doing that you dislike, that have no connection to somewhere you want to go and that are causing you to miss amazing and valuable experiences.

Questions are powerful things.

Where you are not, is as important as where you are.

Why You Should Move Away from Your Hometown

"A prophet is honored everywhere except in his own hometown and among his relatives and his own family." – Mark 6:4

You want to grow, progress, live an interesting and meaningful life. You want to do and be something big, by your own definition. You want the freedom to explore and dive deep into what interests you and maybe even master a few things. You want to know yourself and most of all esteem yourself.

If that's true – and I hope it is – you need to move away from your hometown.

You can always go back later if you want, but if you never leave you'll always be contained within strictures not of your own making. At home you're always only an outgrowth of your perceived past.

In another place you're that wild outsider with intriguing ideas and a fiery passion for life. In your hometown you're little Jimmy, Bev and Stan's kid.

In a new town you're the girl who's full of promise. You can define yourself, write your story, let your first impression speak for itself. Anything you do is potentially interesting and you can potentially be successful in any endeavor. Back home you're the kid who wanted to be a vet when she was 12 and to many people, anything you do other than that will be seen as a compromise.

In a new city your value must come from what you can produce. You are judged and evaluated on your merits, by your fruit. In your hometown you're loved and cute and special no matter what you do, but never fully respected as an independent being.

It's hard to discover yourself when you're defined so much by your heritage, perceptions others have formed about your family and their place, and your past selves.

People from where I grew up still ask me if I'm going to be President some day. Nothing could be more repulsive to me than the idea of running for political office. I wouldn't wish office on my worst enemy and I think politics is the most backward form of human activity and energy. But once upon a time I thought politics was a viable method for expanding human freedom. I told people around me about it. That's the me they knew. To them, I will never be successful or interesting unless and until I achieve a goal that is totally meaningless to me now.

Even if you care about your hometown and want to improve it, the best way is to leave.

Outsiders are more likely to innovate. This is true in all fields. The most likely to have a breakthrough in one industry is not the industry expert or insider but the expert from a different sector who's looking in with fresh eyes.

I once heard that the definition of an expert as someone who has traveled more than 150 miles to deliver a message. Introduce a speaker from next door and, no matter how much they know about the topic at hand, few will be moved and impressed. Fly someone in from the next city and they'll get attention no matter what they say.

Leave.

Go out into the world and discover who you are. Not who you were when your imagination was limited. Not what you grew up thinking and wanting. Not what your family or friends thought about you. You needn't reject or be angry with any of them. You simply need to do what they don't know how to help you do: grow into something beyond the confines of your point of origin.

Go out and become what you want to be and you'll discover something interesting if you go back home. You'll have a level of respect and influence and freedom you could never have won had you stayed.

You're not just somebody's kid. You're somebody. Be you.

Why Kids Do What Their Parents Do

Why do so many children follow in their parents' professional footsteps?

Investigate professional sports, or entertainment, or entrepreneurship, and you'll find a large percentage of those making a living there had parents who did the same. I do not discount the role played by heredity. Nor do I overlook the effects of learning from parents how to ply the craft, or connections parents can provide. But I think there's something else going on as well. Kids who grow up with parents that do X do not feel the need to seek permission to pursue a career in X.

If I asked you, in all seriousness, if you wanted to change life direction and become a rock star you'd probably laugh. You'd laugh because you see rock star as something outside the realm of possibility for you. Even if you have some musical interest or talent, you'd feel sheepish about attempting to reach rock star status. You'd probably want to hone your skills in private for a considerable time before unveiling them to the world. Even then rock star might seem too distant a target.

But I bet your response would be different if you had a parent who was a rock star. Even if you'd not spent much time on music or asked your rock star parent for advice and connections, you'd view a music career as a real possibility.

The things you've seen people close to you do are possible. They are matter of fact things that don't seem all that lofty. Kids who grow up around actors aren't embarrassed to make headshots or go to auditions. Kids with athlete parents aren't intimidated by tryouts or the idea of being team captain. I suspect it's more for this reason than pure nepotism that even mediocre performers often have careers in entertainment when they're related to a star. They simply don't fear the things required to step out and give it a try.

Most kids feel the need to ask for permission to pursue big dreams. It's almost as if they think they need to be invited or discovered. If you've never seen someone who does it except on TV, it might seem too far-off. If you're familiar with it, it automatically becomes a part of your set of options and you need no one's permission to pursue it.

The first hurdle to doing anything is knowing you don't need permission. Bring your heroes down to earth. Remember they're also fallible, searching people. Imagine what their kids must think of them, as kids always see the weak and mundane side as well as the great. Expand your set of options beyond the familiar; or rather, make all options familiar.

Leaving Your Parents' Nest

Most parents mean well. Many are even unconscious of their own forms of manipulation and if revealed to them, they'd prefer to change it.

If you are to create a meaningful and enjoyable life you must break the power of parental control. It's a massive psychological burden and it's sapping your energy, freedom, and fun.

I knew a guy once who dated two very different girls. At some point in both relationships, things became pretty serious. Maybe this was going to be a long-term thing.

In the first relationship the girl was smitten but her parents were not. Not even close. They did not approve of her dating this guy and they made that clear. Things were icy.

He'd go with her for family holidays and it always ended the same. Afterwards, she'd cry and share with him how hard it was to have them so unhappy with her choice. Even if he wasn't there, every time she'd visit home this guy knew there would be fallout when she came back. She'd confide in him just how much it meant to have her parent's approval of the relationship. This put tremendous pressure on him to live up to some standard that lived in her parents' heads.

The relationship eventually ended. It wasn't too pretty either. Yet, time passed and he eventually began dating someone seriously again.

In the second relationship, much like the first, the girl was smitten but her parents were not. Not even close. They did not approve of her dating this guy and they made that clear. Here we go again, he thought. He was nervous. He knew he couldn't take another situation like the last. But this time things never got icy.

The very first time his girlfriend's father voiced his displeasure she said, *"This is who I'm dating. This is who I want to be with. If you want me in your life you're going to have to accept the choices that I make."*

Her dad did not disown her. Instead, he chose to overcome his own prejudice and work to get to know they guy. He did. Today, they're in-laws.

Consciously or unconsciously, parents can sense your need for their approval. The stronger and more desperate it is, the more leverage they have to control you. But the thing is, your parents don't actually possess that leverage in reality. They want to have a relationship with you just as much or more than you do with them, and this feeling increases as they age. That's why if you are definite in your purpose and you make that clear to them, nine times out of ten they will see your earnest resolve and adapt to it.

This makes knowing who you are and what you really want paramount. If you're unsure you'll just end up issuing a constant stream of threats to your parents, which isn't healthy for anybody. However, if you really know what you want; and you are fully prepared to live the consequences with or without your parent's support; and you can calmly and clearly let them know; then they are very likely to end up supporting you.

You don't need to disown them. Just let them know their threat to disown you will not stop you.

They're not as stubborn as they may seem when it comes down to it. They want you to be happy, and if it's clear that you will only be happy pursuing things your own way – and you're aware of the risk and willing to take it – they'll stop trying to resist you.

There is no amount of parental approval that's worth your dignity, freedom, and power as an individual.

Hanging Out with People Your Age is Overrated

There are obvious benefits to building a social circle of people in the same age range. Shared aesthetics and cultural touchstones, similar stages in life that provide better understanding, and similar energy levels are all a few examples.

Still, a network of similarly aged people is overrated.

It's overrated because almost everyone talks about social life as if it is not only preferable among same-aged peers, but impossible with anyone else. People assume that if you move to a city or company or join a church or club without a large population of people your age you will be incapable of building a social life. This lack of open-mindedness and creativity is disturbing, and you can shortchange yourself if you adopt it.

It's not easy to see beyond your age group because most of us spent the first 20-plus years of life bound exclusively to those within 12 months of our own age, outside a few parents, teachers, and others who were always in "authority" positions and never seen as equals in our network. I'm amazed how foreign many schooled kids consider the prospect of hanging out with someone even just a few years their younger or elder. I'm also amazed at how little adults interact with children or the elderly through the course of everyday life, not just on holidays and special occasions.

It's not morally bad to associate exclusively with people your age, and you have no duty to do otherwise. It's simply impractical and limits both the value and enjoyment of your network.

The ability to build an age-diverse social circle is not only for professional network richness, it's also great for personal happiness. The kind of person who can comfortably hang out at a cocktail party of people half or twice their age is someone who will be more interesting and interested in life in general. If your social scene is built around shared excitement, rather than shared station in life – often an artifact of a stodgy, top-down, centrally-planned, education-career conveyor belt – you'll be ridiculously adaptable and quick to connect wherever you go.

Don't succumb to hopelessness or frustration if you move somewhere or work somewhere without a lot of people your age. See it as an opportunity to connect with fascinating people from all stages and stations in life. You'll always be able to (at least superficially) connect with people your age. It's an easy fallback and can sometimes make you lazy about building deeper connections. The chance to create a vibrant social life that's far more diverse is one you should seize as a challenge and a game with big rewards if you don't give up.

Invite someone over who's well outside your age range but whom you find fascinating. Ask yourself if similar people would invite you over just for fun. If not, get working on it.

A Key to Better Conversation with Anyone

There's a script for new interactions we've been programmed to rehearse. It happens on autopilot.

It's goes something along these lines: *"Oh, hi. It's nice to meet you, so what do you do?"*

On many occasions, I've caught myself regurgitating these words like lines from a play. It's not from superficial interested, either. It's something more Pavlovian than that. It's the response we've been conditioned to recite for years, as if we're all merely products defined by our roles in society, rather than humans with passions, a family, and a story.

It happens all around us, and it walks with us through each stage in our lives. Questions about what you wanted to be morphed into questions about your major, where you went to school, or some other classifying information. Whatever the question, the result is the same, and I'm guilty of it, too.

I call it qualifying by classifying, and it's really an easy recipe. You take a glassful of notions about an individual, add two shots of answers to surface-level questions, stir in a pinch of prejudice, garnish with a stereotype, stir, and then drink up this mind-numbing libation. Add rash judgment according to your preference.

This isn't healthy, and it does not serve us well in our pursuits of achieving more fulfillment from life. Instead, it continues a broken narrative that our existence is pointless. It supports a groupthink mentality that our own intrinsic, individual characteristics don't matter. It adds to the propagation of society as a swarm of worker bees, beholden to the hive. It grants us each a label according to our role–rather than our personality–as if it's our duty–rather than our choice.

But, there is still hope.

It happens by working on our delivery. Instead of asking someone what they do, ask, *"What's your story?"* or *"What keeps you up at night?"* or even, *"What do you like to do on Sundays?"*

The goal is simple. Find out wake makes a person tick. Find out what makes them come alive. Watch the fire light in their eyes when you change the narrative.

People love talking about themselves, detailing their passions, and telling their stories. What they likely don't get often is someone eager to listen. This is not mere conjecture. Research has proven the areas of the brain that respond to self-disclosure are also associated with reward. People really, truly, love talking about themselves.

Here's the beauty of this, though. When you engage someone else this way and set them into motion about their story, you will learn more about them than you would by asking them what they do or about their major. Why? Because when you show interest, it allows others to let down their guard and make way for a friendly conversation. Before you know it, you'll be figuring out how your aunts went to high school together or planning a cookout.

But why does it even matter?

Here's why. Because a lot of people haven't thought out what makes them happy or evaluated what they would do differently if they could. They're just like you and me, moving through life, searching for answers, only to find more questions. But something happens when someone engages us and we get to talking. The wheels start turning and it awakens feelings and inspirations that we've either repressed or forgotten about. Sometimes, all someone needs is to feel like they have the permission to let it all out. We can do that for other people, and it doesn't even cost a thing.

Once upon a time, a stranger asked me what made me come alive. He asked me about my goals and my ideal life, where I envisioned myself in a few years, and why it all mattered to me. It floored me. I thought this guy was the most impressive person I'd ever spoken to. Why? Because he made me feel like a rock star. He challenged me to provide answers to questions I had not even articulated for myself. He took more than a surface level interest, and he listened intensely.

I walked away from that conversation remembering him. I remembered how he made me feel, too. And I couldn't shake the questions. They stuck with me. So, over the course of several weeks following that conversation, I hashed out answers to a lot of those questions. All of this from just a simple conversation that only took a few minutes of a stranger's time.

Now, I'm not proposing you do this as charity. You can approach it from a motive of self-interest. You can even look at it as a key for networking better and making people remember you. You can do it from the joy you'll likely receive from witnessing someone light up as they describe their story to you. You can do it to feel like a good person.

It doesn't really matter why you choose to, or even if you choose to at all. But, I assure you, you're leaving value on the table in every interaction you have if you're continuing to engage people solely based upon their occupation or education. You could instead capitalize on that missed value.

Give it a shot. It might require some practice. Undoing years of socially cultivated colloquial usually does. But don't be afraid to change the narrative. What's the worst that could happen?

Want to Be Interesting? Be Interested

Interesting people differ from each other in so many ways. In fact, one of the things that makes a person interesting is how little like others they are. Those who embrace their unique weirdness, not in a flashy attempt for attention but as a secure mode of being, tend to be very interesting. Still, it's not the truly unique qualities about interesting people that make them interesting. It's something they all have in common.

They are interested.

An interesting writer, artist, entrepreneur, academic, or cook is someone who has not only mastered a craft, but someone deeply, intensely interested in their craft. The mastery typically follows the interest. What's more, interesting people are not only interested in what they do and what they have mastered. They're interested in just about everything in the world. They aren't afraid to be in awe of the world around them, from the big philosophical questions to the tiny details.

I used to do fundraising for a nonprofit and my favorite part was meetings with incredibly successful, self-made people who almost always began as average people, and somehow built amazing companies and products and lives. I'd ask their stories and soak up all the details of their founding saga; how they got into that industry, why they chose to live where they did, and so on. What stuck out was that, happy as they were to discuss these things, most of them were equally excited to talk about a style of painting they were fond of, the aerodynamics of aircraft, logo design, and in one case the habits of ants. These were interesting people because they were interested people.

I once heard an anecdote about a young boy who told his grandfather that he was bored. Calmly, his grandfather rolled up a magazine, leaned over, and whacked the boy on the head. *"Bored people grow up to become boring people."* With no TV or laptop or iPhone or books or friends around, would you be bored? Or could you find a way to engage the world around and within you no matter where you were and what tools you had? Those who have mastered the art of the latter are never boring.

We're surrounded by wonders, great and small, easy to spot and almost impossible to find. Can you sense it? Do you feel it? Do you have questions about it? As G.K. Chesterton said, *'we don't lack wonders, we lack wonder.'*

Fearing Sameness vs. Fearing Difference

There are a lot of cultural memes about accepting people who are different and embracing diversity of all kinds. But I wonder if it's actually harder to tolerate sameness than difference.

Consider people or ideas that cause the most upheaval. They are often those that reveal the depth of sameness and lack of distinction in culture, rather than radical difference. Tell someone an English degree is more worthless than a Math degree. You'll rile some people up, but it will mostly be a playful rivalry. The distinction between these two degrees allows people to set themselves apart and sometimes argue, but both feel fairly secure in their unique place. But say that all degrees, no matter what area of study, are essentially the same and that the believed differentiation is a farce, and you'll have a lot of angry people on your hands.

Likewise, there are always people who favor one religion and smear another. They point to sharp contrasts between the beliefs and values of different religious texts and traditions. Society can tolerate them and they're not really threatening at the core. The greatest heretics are those who claim that all religions are equally true or equally false. The removal of cherished uniqueness, the revelation of sameness and, lack of distinction threatens the very fabric of society.

People can tolerate difference. They have categories for it. They can tolerate hierarchy and the occasional odd one out. They are scared to death of sameness. They are terrified of discovering they're really a lot more like their neighbor next door or in a distant land than they are different.

The paradox is that most people strive for sameness. They want their kid to be average, and they want to be average. That's why almost everyone thinks they are middle class. They don't want to stick out on either tail of the bell curve. They strive for it, but they don't dare admit it.

The great mutual secret of society is sameness. We believe great distinctions and huge divides exist between people and ways of life. We don't speak of the sameness. The great times of crisis are when differences fade. Rich and poor alike are decimated by economic collapse. Flood and earthquakes are indiscriminate. The break-down of perceived and real differences is perhaps more frightening and threatening to our culture than anything.

Don't Do It to Feel Normal

Most people don't go to college to learn. That can be done much easier and less costly in myriad other ways.

Most people don't go to college to become well-rounded. That can happen through any number of experiences.

Most people don't go to pick a career. They could try working some different jobs to learn quicker, and most don't work in what they major in anyway.

Most don't go for the practical value of the credential. I've never met a college student who actually inquired with employers what they view as the best credential.

Most people don't even go to college for the social experience. How many examine all the ways to meet people, party, etc. and firmly conclude college is the best way for them to have fun?

Most people go to college to be normal.

It's the normal thing. They want to meet normal people, make normal friends, learn normal facts, have normal experiences, and appear normal to family, friends, and future employers. They take it on faith that college is good, beneficial, educational, career-enhancing, a great social experience, worth the cost, etc., rather than really examine these oft repeated tropes. They want them to be true because they want to list these normal reasons for doing what's normal.

College can be great. Besides, it's too late for most of us to consider alternatives. But if you are pre-college, ask yourself what you really want out of it. Look long and hard at other ways to get what you want. Weigh the costs. Be prepared if you find college is not the best way...you may discover your best path is not normal.

Are you ready and willing to bear the social costs of an abnormal choice? It might be worth it.

Your Student Debt Is Unfair

You hear a lot of complaints about student debt, and how maddening it is to be $40,000 in the hole at age 23 and still not have a job that requires a degree. The case for the unfairness of student loan debt is that these kids didn't know better. It's kind of a pathetic excuse, but it's often true.

Twelve years in an education system being constantly pummeled with the promises of higher education and the perils of any deviation will make you overvalue a degree. You'll never be warned about the cost, or how debt can limit your options. You'll only be told about the magic $1 million in lifetime earnings that is supposed to find you as soon as you find your major and graduate.

It's a system. Obey it, and the statistics will magically bring you what they brought the average of the past aggregate, as long as your behavior correlates with theirs.

Starry eyed teens get grants, aid, scholarships, loans, and complete a bunch of paperwork with their parents just to get in to the best possible college they can based on rankings they've never really studied. They get endless praise upon graduation and more upon heading off to college. Finally, they've made it! The rest of life will simply unfold successfully as if on autopilot. What's the worst that could happen now? You're getting a degree, so you're set! You're on the right side of the data!

Young people get good enough grades, do some extracurriculars, and get a degree. Once more they are celebrated. Then, for perhaps the first time in 20 years, they leave the confines of a controlled environment shielded from the world of value creation and exchange.

No one is overly impressed with their ability to fit into the system anymore. People want to know what they bring to the table. Can they crunch meaningful numbers without being assigned? Can they sell? Can they code? Can they digest the complexities of markets and customers and make judgments on the fly about how to preempt problems? Not really. Those things take experience and context wholly lacking in most educational institutions.

So they struggle. They don't like what they do, or they can't find work much better than what they could have gotten right out of high school. It's OK though, they have time to learn from the real world right? Except they've got college debt to pay—in addition to living expenses. That awesome company they were going to volunteer for in order to gain skills? Not so easy with the need to earn enough to make loan payments.

Grads are in a bind and they feel kind of ripped off. They feel betrayed. They feel lied to. Where is that high school guidance counselor who pushed them to college? Will she pay the bills? Where are the parents who were so proud? Will they want their kid to move back home? It can be pretty rough.
So yes, it's unfair. But the worst possible way to respond and improve things is to say it's unfair over and over. Say it once, get it out of your system, and move on. The fairness doesn't matter.

Sometimes you'll act on bad information. Sometimes you'll have regrets. Sometimes other people's plans for you aren't best and you'll suffer for following them. So what? Talking about how sad or unfair it is does nothing but reduce the chances that you'll actually make things better.

Yes, you were most likely led to believe your degree would pay for itself immediately and without difficulty. Yes, because you were handicapped by the system you were incapable of realizing for yourself what the decision to go into debt might mean and how it could play out. That's the past. What will you do today?

The good news is it's not that big of a deal unless you let it be. Laugh at it, roll up your sleeves, and reboot your expectations about the world while building every day. Devise a payoff plan and a life improvement plan. Lots of people have done it, and so can you. The past is past, you are where you are, and no amount of bitterness, protest, or hoping for some political savior to bail you out will do you good. In fact, it might destroy you.

Oh, and if you have kids of your own someday, let them experience enough of the world outside the walls of schools so that they know better than to blindly follow the advice of authorities seeking to do them good.

A Degree Won't Make You Rich(er)

Many students are being duped into believing myths of a causal relationship existing between higher education and upward mobility. It's long past time purveyors of this perverse notion carefully reassess their commentary.

At best, it is an inaccurate assessment of reality. At worst, it is a fatal error. It's naive to assume a degree determines equity or value in the marketplace. A degree, much like a driver's license, is no more than a signal. Just as a license does not indicate ability to drive, a college degree indicates no special aptitude for performing tasks necessary to earn a wage. Each serves as an emblem, neither as a guarantee.

Unfortunately, many young people are marinated in this unhealthy distortion of reality for 15,000+ hours before being released into the great big world to investigate for themselves. It's hardly a surprise so many choose to pursue a college degree. From a young age, I too heard the fiery sermons about going to college to ensure landing a good job. I heard all about how degree holders, on aggregate, make over $1M more than non-degree holders.

Sadly, I bought into the lies.

I went off and I earned my college degree. Thankfully I only wasted four years. During this prison sentence I realized how inadequate institutions of higher education are at determining a person's ability to earn an income.

I'm not one who sits still and classrooms are the bane of my existence. So I skipped most of my classes while there. I still did well on the homework and was an ace at examinations, but my poor attendance cost me many top marks. No skin off my nose. My real education while at college was hard-earned on my own beyond the confines of cinderblock cells. It's outside the classroom where I learned to create value for others.

My senior year of college, I might as well have dropped out. Looking back I wish I had. I wasted a lot of time trying to skate by as the end neared. My periphery compliance prevented me from giving more attention to my interests. I could've gained more from that time.

For instance, I launched my freelance career that year. I also bartered with a handful of other students to complete their assignments or take entire courses for them. Each moment I spent in the classroom withdrew time and effort I could have better spent growing these businesses. I learned far more from both of these activities than I ever did in a classroom.

I also learned from these transactions that many people don't give a shit about the education element of higher education. Most inherently recognize that it's only a signal, not an indicator of skill. They'd be content simply purchasing the signal if it was possible. But heaven forbid they forego four years of revelry. What's sadder yet is that many young people can't formulate a decent response as to why they've chosen to pursue a degree. They've never flipped the burden of proof.

Many of the reasons, if challenged, would better justify simply moving to a college town for four years, finding a job, and foregoing school altogether.

Challenging the Narrative

While the reasons for seeking a degree are as many and varied as are the institutions ready to provide one, the number of young people amassing crippling debt burdens is even greater. Young people are being cheated. Not (only) by lenders and the government, but also by a fraudulent education system. The product these institutions market is not what it claims to be. In most cases, I'd even argue the product is harmful to the wellbeing of its consumers. Sadly, it's more a feature of the system than a flaw of it.

The folklore of the institution of education pretends otherwise: "Attend school as long as possible. Make stellar grades. Listen to the teachers and professors. Get a good job. Don't worry about what it costs. Your education is the best investment you could ever make."

This narrative is bullshit.

For one, it's a blanket statement applied gratuitously to every student in every circumstance. Rarely would you ever hear a guidance counselor tell a student he or she should consider making different plans after high school. This isn't unfair. It's unrealistic. Some people are not cut out for the classroom–I might even argue that most aren't.

For those who can manage to learn inside the borders of a class, assuming that college is always the best option is dishonest. In many cases the cost of obtaining a higher degree comes at much too high a toll. The debt can be paralyzing and the incessant ranking against peers demoralizing. Furthermore, the authoritarian exposition in which most formal education is set harmfully stifles creativity and originality of many of its brightest pupils. Some young people would be best to pursue learning on their own terms.

Speaking of learning. The institution of education presumes good grades and obedience to the pedagogy equates to an understanding of subject matter. Again, this is erroneous. In some cases it might be true. But it is certainly not true of every student in every case. Speak not of cheating, but the academic system as structured encourages rote memorization and rewards those who best regurgitate material. This diminishes the incentives of developing sound logic skills, of challenging the status quo, and of discovering answers for oneself.

With all this emphasis on grades and obedience and little demand for providing real social proof of an attained skill or prowess in an area of study, the school releases these young, barren minds into the world on the job hunt. Saturated with lofty ideals and a sense of entitlement cultivated by years of promise that arriving at that this moment would pay dividends, receiving a diploma often marks the pride before the fall.

It's no wonder many young people walk around jaded and plagued by despair. They're not much different than many millions who have lost it all in the stock market on speculation. Except in rare circumstances, every adversary the young people ever had egged them on to push all their chips in on college. At least with the stock market there's an air of skepticism that goes with the territory.

The narrative of college also fails to critically engage young people in thinking about what they could do instead. This is perhaps the most grotesque error. The advent of technology has put an instruction manual on any possible skill in the pocket of every young person. What young people need instead of college is experience. College takes away time and focus from gaining meaningful experience. It also presumes that the degree is a more valuable signal than the experience that could have been gained in the same amount of time. I caution this thinking.

There are also many other classic arguments like: "You need college because you're no Bill Gates, Steve Jobs, or Mark Zuckerberg."

I say great. The world might not need another Microsoft, Apple, or Facebook. Most people don't have revolutionary ideas, but they do possess revolutionary points of view. It also might be intellectually lazy to set the status of 'billionaire mogul' as a standard of success of foregoing college or dropping out. Their stories still provide useful examples though, even if–especially if–you don't have a revolutionary idea.

Here's why. You don't have to have a revolutionary idea to forego college. You just need to figure out what people want and how to deliver that to them. This is where your revolutionary point of view will come in handy. Whether those people you're providing value for are potential employers, consumers, customers, friends, or anyone. Create and sell what people want, and you'll always have whatever you need. You don't necessarily have to provide exceptional products. You have to provide products or services that people want, exceptionally. And this doesn't require a degree.

Some other examples

There are rappers, musicians, artists, athletes, writers, chefs, business owners, and even eight U.S. presidents who don't (or didn't) have college degrees. You don't need one either. Learn to recognize what people want or could use. Figure out a way to get it to them at a price they're willing to pay. That's all. If you can figure that out then all of college and higher education is obsolete.

But what if I'm studying business?

You won't get business acumen in the classroom. College as a prerequisite to business acumen is a myth MBA-types and elitists cower behind. They lurk behind their lofty suffixes because deep down they're afraid of the truth. The truth that their time and effort was all for not. That it was wasted. That they could have obtained it better, cheaper, or faster. I pity those who entertain this mindset for their lack of intellectual depth. Somewhere in their pasts, someone must have eradicated their imaginations. They are no longer humans, but computers. They've traded in their outside the box thinking for algorithms and actuarial science. They've given up sentient thought.

If they had any imagination, they could fathom abstract like success and achievement as existing outside a vacuum. They could recognize that income potential and upward mobility are not static ideas, but fluid, ever-changing enigmas with subjectively calculated value. Degrees are no different.

A Degree's Value is Subjective

Just because the world says a degree is worth a lot doesn't mean potential employers will care. It also doesn't mean it will necessarily make a person feel more successful or happier. Much like a bottle of water is worth more than a diamond to a thirsty man in the desert, the ability to create value is worth immensely more to an employer than a degree–even an ivy league one.

Today, obtaining a college degree is easier than it ever has been. That's what makes it so dangerous to tout its value and necessity. It's simple supply and demand, or call it degree inflation. The more people that have a degree, the less value it holds to differentiate you in the marketplace.

Because of the massive influx, the signal that a degree once held has dwindled from a flare to an ember. If you want to distinguish yourself, a degree is a poor mechanism for doing so. You could use some social proof or a value proposition instead. You could use experience or a skill set. You could use any number of things as a better signal–even if you want to use these in conjunction with a college education–but don't fool yourself that the degree alone is sufficient.

So, say you feel like college is not for you. How do you go about creating a better signal?

Simple. Here's one method I propose:

Make a short list of a handful of things that interest you. Whatever they are, write them down. Don't be afraid to go big.

Next, make a short list of things you are good at. Not just things your mom tells you you're good at. What things would everyone you know say you're good at?

If any of the items on these two lists merge then congratulations. You've found a starting point. You are now equipped to find a business owner who has a need for a service that lives at the intersection of your interests and skills. When you find said business owner, ask if you can shadow him or her for a week or more. If this is granted, do it ASAP. Take notes. Learn everything you can and constantly assess ways your skills could add value to the operation.

At the end of the shadowing, first, draft a thank you note to the business owner. Along with it, draft a proposal on how your unique interests and skills could be engaged valuably to the business owner. From what you learned about the business in shadowing, detail what you witnessed. "The following areas could benefit from innovation, and I'm just the person to do it."

Why? Because you want to learn and improve his or her enterprise and at your age you need experience more than money. Do not pitch your skills. Do not pitch your financial situation. Meditate on the business owner's vision and pitch your desire to help achieve it.

When you're hired, as you most likely will be, and begin working to fulfill this agreement, document your work. Build a portfolio as you go of the projects you create—if the info isn't sensitive. Start a blog or build a quick website to host the things you learn and to feature the projects you create. Boom. You'll never have to worry about a degree again.

To all the young people out there who have fallen victim to statistics and the social commentary about college, don't fret. The same opportunity is open to you. While your limited availability might impact your prospect to gain real experience, openness to ideas, a strong work ethic, a hunger to learn and unswerving dependability can help you overcome that.

Ultimately, it's your life.

Whether you choose to pursue a college education or not is entirely up to you. Don't make a blind decision. Be mindful of the opportunities you're foregoing and the time, effort, and money you might be wasting. Don't rely on a degree as a signal of your worth. Create a better one.

When It's Good to Be A Failure

I'm a failure according to my own definition.

The current me doesn't think I'm a failure – I'm pretty happy about where I'm at in life and feel I'm doing what I love at the moment. It's one of the versions of me from the past that thinks I'm a failure.

There was a time when I thought being an elected politician was the way to live and spread freedom. I went to work in the legislature to see how to become a lawmaker. During that time I met a lot of people who didn't know me before and haven't kept up since. They knew the Isaac who defined success as being an elected official. Friends and relatives saw me working in politics and could foresee what a successful end in that realm looked like in their minds. For these people, my life won't be a success until I achieve what I was then pursuing.

Along the way I learned more about myself. My goals didn't change, just the way I visualized achieving them. I was pursuing a certain ideal and a bundle of sensations. I was pursuing freedom. I was incapable of imagining anything but a crude vision of political freedom, and my worldview was so simple I thought politicians created it. Therefore I wanted to be one. Freedom is still what I wanted, but with more experience and knowledge I came to believe being involved in politics would be the worst possible way to achieve it. My definition of success morphed.

This happens all the time with humans. A child may say he wants to be a firefighter only because in his world, firefighter is one of the four or five options he can imagine. It's the one that makes him feel the most excited and good about helping people.

As they grow, children learn about a huge range of activities in the world and realize that, to achieve the feeling they desire, firefighting is an inferior method to being a paramedic, a teacher, an entrepreneur, or an X-Games athlete. It's not that we sell out on our dreams, it's just that our dreams were crude representations of what we thought we wanted. When we learn more, we make different decisions.

C.S. Lewis talks about the, *"[I]gnorant child who wants to go on making mud pies in a slum because he cannot imagine what is meant by the offer of a holiday at the sea."*

Once we learn what's possible, we laugh at what we previously thought of as the ultimate achievement. This growth is all well and good until we confront people from our past who have us locked in to our previous dreams.

Sometimes people ask me when I'm going to be president, and no matter what answer I give, it seems to them like a cop-out or excuse for my own failure. They refuse to believe me when I say I wouldn't wish political office on my worst enemy, let alone myself. They think I'm being modest.

I have a friend who went to Hollywood wanting to be an actor and now realizes his creative energies are far broader. People back home always want to know when they'll see him on the big screen. We sometimes joke that someday, when he has millions and is producing, directing, writing and doing whatever he wants in life, his friends back home will say, *"Haven't seen you on TV...you just haven't caught that break yet, huh?"*

It can be a little weird to describe how and why your dreams and definitions of success change over time. A lot of people don't actually want to know. They just want to know if you're Governor yet, or an Oscar winning actor. That's all right. Don't fret over it and don't spend too much energy trying to convince them you're really not a failure. If they insist on defining success the way you did before you knew better, just let them think you're a failure and laugh at the absurdity.

If I'm a failure for not being the silly thing I once wanted to be, it's good to be a failure.

You Can Afford to Fail

"I can't afford to fail." A young person recently told me this. He was deciding whether to try something he was really excited about, but that was new and different, and not even particularly risky. He sincerely meant it. It was clear he saw this as a make-or-break moment in his life, and it broke my heart. You can afford to fail. In fact, you can't afford to avoid failure.

I'm not sure all the causes, though I believe schooling is a very deep part of the root system, but young people are terrified of failure. It's completely backwards. Never in human history has there been such a soft landing. Never has it been easier to recover. When a business or an event or a project fails, it doesn't mean you fail. In fact, a failed business can be the surest path to personal success, if you don't let it ruin you.

Failure is not catastrophic. It's just a part of the process of success. You try to ride a bike and you fall down. You try to play video games and you lose. Kids seem able to recover from failure at these pretty easily. Maybe because their parents don't care and don't show anxiety and anger and send them into remedial video game classes and summer camps. Whatever the reason, there's something to be taken from these failures. Apply that same nonchalance to life. Life is nothing but a series of games.

The desire to succeed and frustration at failure is normal and can be productive and motivating, but only when you're doing something you know you want to be doing. The real killer is crippling fear of failing at some arbitrary standard set by someone else, or fear of what other people will think even when you don't really care about the end goal itself. When exploring and learning something new, failure is to be expected. Don't internalize it. Learn from it, laugh at it, and move on.

One you've gained some level of mastery, then competitive pressure and desire to be perfect can be helpful. I once read about a study where pool players were observed. When they were told they were being observed and judged the amateur pool players started playing a lot worse. The really good players started playing better. We need a lot of judgment free space to explore, learn, and decide what we like and get better at it. Self-judgment needs to be the first to go. After you've mastered something you can choose to take failure personally if it helps you and motivates you, but not before.

I think a lot of people are scared of entrepreneurship because they hear statistics about what percent of new businesses fail. But notice what's happening here. You hear that a business failed, and in your mind you subtly converge the business with the founder and assume that the founder failed. You assume if you start a business odds say it will fail, and therefore you will fail and you don't want to fail. But that's not what happens. When a business fails the people involved don't fail. They typically walk away with some great experience, knowledge, new connections, sometimes even money.

Purge your fear of failure. Stop worrying about being average or above average on some arbitrary scale created by someone besides yourself. Freely explore, try things, learn things, and get better at the stuff you love.

You've got to stop avoiding failure if you want to succeed.

Be discerning.
Choose "it" because you want "it".
Do "it" because you want to.

Fear of Success Is Real, Too

The stoic approach has a lot going for it.

Contrary to "name it and claim it", Law of Attraction kind of practices, stoicism admonishes not to fill your head with visions of utopia. It takes the opposite tack.

Mentally explore the worst-case scenario and familiarize yourself with it. This prepares you emotionally to handle whatever comes. By preparing for the worst you'll be unshakeable when anything less occurs.

It's a valuable life philosophy for dealing with fear of failure. When you've already experienced failure mentally and realized it's not all the bad, you gain a certain kind of invincibility not devoid of reason and realism.

But failure is not the only fear that holds us back. Fear of success is a thing too.

What if you launch your blog or produce your movie or sell your new product and it actually takes off? What if you go viral? What if you have more demand than you can keep up with? What if people start writing news stories about you? What if your success presents you with the decision of whether to quit your day job and redefine yourself? What if you threaten the status quo? What if people start suing you? What if people write articles about how much you suck?

What if all your acquaintances start asking you for jobs and money and favors? What if big investors want to fund you but only if you move to a new city? What if the once-quiet evenings at home with your loved ones and Netflix become impossible to maintain along with your new endeavor?

If you really succeed some of these things will happen. They are at least as scary as failure and the stoic approach might cause you to avoid imagining them ahead of time. It's arrogant to close your eyes and feel the experience of wild success, right? It's delusional and might keep you from being able to handle failure, right? Maybe if that's all you ever imagine.

On the flip side, if you're only ever braced for failure you might be blindsided by success and crumble, or worse yet, never go hard after it due to latent fear of its unknown rewards and challenges.

One of those cheesy evangelical phrases I grew up around is pretty accurate here. *"Another level another devil"*. Maybe now your problems and fears loom large. If you don't get the job you won't know how to pay rent. Yet if you succeed in a big way your problems and fears become more, not less serious. If you don't land the deal you'll have to fire thirteen good employees and they won't know how to pay rent. Success can be scary stuff.

If the stoic experience of mentally living through the worst-case is the antidote to fear of failure then I suggest the opposite is the antidote to fear of success.

Envision your best-case scenario. Envision having millions of fans or dollars. Envision wild success and its attendant obligations and challenges. Really, seriously explore what you would do right now if you had it. It presents more challenges than most are willing to acknowledge.

I don't know about the effectiveness of envisioning your goals as a way to achieve them, but I still think it's important to envision success as a way to overcome your fear of it.

The Cure Is Not the Cause

A friend worked at a company that instituted a no cell phone policy during meetings. Apparently too many people were on their phones instead of paying attention.

If you look at it from an authoritarian standpoint as an organizer, the cause for lack of engagement was cell phone use. But put yourself in the shoes of an attendee and you see that cell phones were not the cause of the problem, but the cure for it. The problem was boredom. The cause was too many or too long or not interesting enough meetings.

We see cures blamed as causes everywhere. Schools routinely blame whatever form of escape, entertainment, distraction, or even real learning that kids conceive to cope with the rigid soul-sucking structure of the system. From a top-down, black-and-white rulers standpoint, the answer is always more bans and more rules.

What would happen instead if we assumed rationality and no malicious intent on the part of the cell phone users or students? What might their behavior reveal about the system or process?

If you run a business you can get mad at customers who don't do what you want all you like, but attacking or placing restrictions on them is not a long term strategy for success in a competitive market. You must try to understand why they aren't doing what you want and adapt your offerings.

When people are looking for an escape don't block the exit. Instead try to learn why they want out in the first place.

Don't Rush Your Ideal Life; Rush Away from Boredom

Relax.

No, seriously. Relax. You're not behind the curve. You're not missing out. You don't need to discover your calling or passion or pick your career or industry right now or next month or next year or in ten years. You're not late. You're not going to be screwed if you don't specialize soon. You haven't lost too much time.

This might sound like odd advice from someone who's always telling people that they don't need to wait to get started on an awesome career.

"Get out of the classroom! Get into the real world! Start building a great career today! Don't wait for permission or hope for opportunity! Create!"

That's the kind of stuff I normally say. And it's all true.

So how can, "Don't rush" and, "Don't wait" be equally true? Because they apply to different things.

If you're bored or unhappy or doing something that will force you to be bored or unhappy in the future, rush to the exit right now. If you know there's something interesting and exciting, rush to start it today.

After exiting the crappy situation don't rush to find the perfect path. If you know what it is, go for it with abandon. If you don't, stop feeling guilty about it. As long as you're not doing stuff you hate you're moving in roughly the right direction and each step you take away from lameness is a step towards greatness, even though greatness remains undefined.

The worst of both worlds is rushing into something you hate because you fear you'll get behind if you don't.

"I hate this school/job, but I have to get started and complete it as soon as possible so that I don't miss out on career opportunities!"

That's ass backwards. Chill out. Slow down. Don't jump into something dull and painful when you don't even know when or how it will result in something great. Run from dreary as fast as you can and when you're free don't rush to find some specific next thing that will prematurely lock you in.

Think about people in terrible romantic relationships. You know the type. After finally exiting via terrible breakup they desperately rush right back into a relationship with the first person they find. *Fear Of Missing Out* is no way to pick a partner and it's no way to plot a path to career and life happiness.

The number of great thinkers, artists, and entrepreneurs who didn't get started until their 40's, 50's or beyond is staggering. The average age of startup founders is 40. And averages don't define you anyway. You could be 60. Who cares?
Run as fast as you can from stuff you hate.

Patiently do interesting things whether or not you get paid for it. Continue this process of whittling away the stuff that doesn't make you feel alive and trying everything interesting with no artificial deadlines or timetables for when you must settle in on something or decide what you want to be when you grow up.

Rush to escape bad.

Don't rush to create perfect. Let it emerge through interesting.

Part II: Create A Life You Love

*We're going to make mistakes.
We have to own them.
then, we have to make amends.
then, we have to move on.*

Come Alive

What's the craziest thing you've ever done?

Think about it for a moment. How many things came to mind? For me it's a laundry list. Most were just plain stupid, but each involved something similar: *risk-taking*.

Even some of the less shitbrained ideas throughout the years required risk to some degree. Though a lot of them exploded in my face, I think back fondly on those times and I remember how alive they made me feel.

Like the time they told us not to throw the party that ended with a visit from half the local police force and a few social host tickets. What a night. I think back to the time a group of friends and I drove out to ding-dong-ditch the house where a "crazy" lived. We ended up getting shot at as we sped away. My heart was in my throat. I think about at least another half-dozen times I shouldn't mention, too. Two words: *pumpkin rolling*.

Now, a word of caution. Don't mistake this as a message to run through the streets ensuing destructive chaos. That's not what I'm suggesting at all.

It's not so much the acts I remember being awesome—most have transmogrified into much bigger fish tales. In fact, I often think back about how stupid and unnecessarily risky some of the shenanigans I pulled were. But what I can't erase from memory is the way each breath tasted in the act of taking risks. Something about the uncertainty awakened my spirit.

It made me come alive.

What I didn't know then was how to replicate the same energy and channel it for good. It took years of searching, observing, and learning. And then one day, I stumbled upon the answer.

The day I made my first legitimate dollar as an entrepreneur I witnessed the whole world in a new light. The experience distinguished a key difference for me between destructive vs. creative risk taking. Instead of searching for new highs from potentially hazardous risks, I discovered an entire new kind of satisfaction. It came from the type of risk-taking that paired my interests with the needs of others, from the type of risk-taking that involved an exchange of value. And I was immediately hooked.

This new way to alter my perception and experience a better world inspired me to take on new risks; personal, professional, emotional, spiritual, and every other kind of challenging risk. The answer existed not only in exchange of my services or talents for money. It relied upon facing the risk of putting my interests, talents, and abilities on examination in the real world.

I was still thrill-seeking, per say, but no longer in a way that worked to my own demise. I wasn't drinking in a good time only to wake up with a hangover. No. I learned to drink in the richness of life itself by identifying the natural incentives at play around me.

By monetizing my interests and hobbies, I no longer needed a job. I could set to work on creating a life, and one I loved, to boot. And set to work I did.

I tried my hand at a number of different activities, hobbies, jobs, and favors asked. I read hundreds of books, blogs, and articles. I journaled, wrote, recorded, and detailed dozens of field experiments. From freelance writing, photography, marketing, and graphic design to financial sales, legal research, inventory management and small business consulting, non-profit think tank work, and business development. I built several websites. I narrated a book. I started a podcast. I blogged every day for a month.

I tried everything that interested me, and I still do.

In addition to an entire toolset of skills, I found meaning, satisfaction from life, and ultimately freedom. I discovered how to live on purpose and as the arbiter of my own fate.

Yet, don't be fooled. It all came at an incredibly high cost.

While I avoided hundreds of thousands of dollars in student debt or a premature mortgage, the non-monetary costs certainly took their toll.

I lost friends. I garnered the judgment of quite a few people I once highly respected. I discarded a once-burgeoning social life. I became the butt of quite a few jokes and rumors about having 'gone off the deep end' circulated. On several occasions I was even asked if I needed professional mental help. The verdict might still be out on that one, but these are all prices I'd pay again happily.

Though certainly not a cakewalk, I can assure you discovering and pursuing what makes me come alive has been worth every ounce of effort.

It's for this reason I advocate so strongly against limiting yourself. Unless you already know you hate something, don't shirk away from new experiences. Embrace them boldly. Don't fear stepping out of the crowd, and don't dismiss your ideas because someone calls them crazy.

March out into the world and try it all. Take risks. Find what makes you come alive and eliminate what doesn't. Author a story worth telling.

The life you've always wanted is waiting for you. Will you go create it?

Are You Living on Purpose?

Humans are not like other earthly creatures. We cannot live for only the biological imperative to survive and procreate. Humans require purpose. Lack of purpose is the greatest disease against which all of humanity must daily fight. It is the one disease that will not and cannot be overcome by advances in medicine.

You can't have purpose on accident.

Our existence is couched in a series of accidents. That we were born, when, where, and to whom are accidents (they were not accidents to our progenitors, but from our own point of view). Our genetic structure is an accident. The first language we hear, and therefore learn, and the first beliefs to which we are exposed, and therefore predisposed to, are accidents. Purpose cannot come from accidents. We do not discover or live with purpose naturally, the way we grow physically.

None of these accidents are good or bad. The simply are. In your exploration and creation of purpose you may find that a meaningful life demands radical differences from the norms and beliefs in which you were raised. You may find that it demands beliefs and norms almost identical to those in which you were raised. Whatever the end result, the one consistent demand is that you choose it. You cannot discover and live a purposeful life by simply following rules handed down to you, taking the path of least resistance, and sitting idly on the conveyor belt you were plopped on. It's not where it takes you that matters as much as who decided to go there. If it was not your decision, you will never find fulfillment from it.

Suffering with and without purpose

Suffering is terrible. It can also be valuable, in the same way the physical sensation of pain is valuable. Without it we would soon die of unattended wounds. Because pain is valuable doesn't mean it's noble or to be sought. Psychological suffering is the same.

To suffer is no noble deed. If the suffering is avoidable it's a worthless or even cowardly thing to suffer. If the suffering is unavoidable your response to it can be heroic. There is nothing heroic about the suffering itself, but heroism can be found in someone who chooses to respond by finding meaning in unavoidable suffering.

Do not mistake your suffering for heroism. If it's at all avoidable, the heroic thing to do is to escape from it. If not, create purpose in it.

There is no right decision

No single decision will give you purpose. Your life is not a series of binary choices with the door on the left leading to meaninglessness and the door on the right leading to purposefulness. What you choose at each juncture of your life matters little compared to the fact that you choose, not someone else. You can't find a perfect version of your purposeful life. You have to create it by the undivided, definite choices you make. Consciously choose to do things you value and find meaningful. Consciously exit those that aren't. It doesn't matter what you choose so much as that you choose. Complaining about a path someone else pushed you down and against which you did not resist will not do.

Purposeful living is a process of exploration, experimentation, feedback, adjustment, and joy in the midst of it. There is no pressure to get it right because there is no right. There is better and worse, as determined by you. It requires self-knowledge and self-honesty to find your own scale of better and worse. It requires courage to abide by it.

Are you the 2%?

At any given moment 98% of us will choose – or rather not choose – to live by default. It is only the 2% who decide with definite purpose to act according to their own wishes who are really living.

How often are you among them?

Live the Life You Want - It's Easier Than You Think

I recently listened to an episode of *The World Wanderers Podcast* where the host discussed working at a Cafe in a great city that a lot of people would love to live in. She mentioned how, had she not moved to this cool, exciting city, the job she had would have made her feel like a loser. In your hometown working retail after getting an expensive degree seems pretty lame. Up and moving to a destination city and working retail to support the lifestyle seems kind of adventurous.

Back home, she would have dreaded seeing an old friend come in. *"Oh, so you're working here?"* In the new city when someone she knew came in the question was more like, *"Wow, so you're living here?"*

Just a few days ago I talked to a guy who's biking across the country and loving it. He spent several months in beautiful Missoula, Montana waiting for the weather to improve so he could continue his journey. He worked at a grocery store while there and it provided everything he needed to live the lifestyle he wanted and get back on the road in time. What would his resume look like when, several years out of college, he had *"Grocery bagger"* listed? Not great, except when put in the context of, *"Spent two years biking across the U.S., paying my way through with odd jobs and blogging about the adventure."*

I thought about this phenomenon more in Mompiche, Ecuador, when my family experimented living there for six weeks. We found a little place with a sign for American-style pancakes; a welcome breakfast after days of fruit and cereal. The breakfast nook was run by a twenty-something woman from the Ukraine. She fried up pancakes on a small griddle and served them with coffee for breakfast and lunch in the tiny Bohemian surfing village. She lived in a neat little house right above the pancake joint and spent the rest of the day as she pleased.

Imagine this ambitious young woman back home responding to the common, *"So, what do you do?"* with, *"I make pancakes for a living."* Likely her friends and family would be a little worried, ashamed, or perhaps think something wrong with her.

Contrast that with the same answer to the same question but with a change in geography. *"I moved across the world to a tropical surfing village in Ecuador where I opened my own business."* Wow. What an enviable life, right?

There's something weird about staying in your hometown. It severely limits the definitions you accept for what makes you successful. Oddly, most of the hometown definitions of success have nothing to do with happiness. They have to do with becoming what everyone in your past expects or desires given who you used to be–like a tether to a past self that no longer exists.

When the expectations of back home no longer apply, you can ask better questions and make clearer connections. What kind of person do you want to be (vs. what job title do you want)? What kind of people and surroundings do you want to be immersed in (vs. where do you want to work or live)?

Many people would probably love to be the master of their own schedule, be in a beautiful outdoor setting with interesting people from around the world, seriously pursue a hobby with lots of their time, and be challenged in new ways daily. Yet most of those same people would be horrified at the idea of playing guitar on the street for money, flipping pancakes, or doing freelance odd-jobs online, any of which might be the very means to achieve the life described.

Most people have this idea that you have to work a boring job in a boring house in a boring city for a few decades, and then if you play your cards right and all kinds of things totally out of your control do the right thing, you can have some kind of two week vacation cruise or retire in a place where you enjoy good weather and leisure.

The weird thing is, all those "someday" goals are available right now with relatively little difficulty. You can afford to live in a cool bamboo house in a beach town just by making pancakes for lunch and breakfast. You can travel the length of South America living entirely off the cash you make playing guitar outside of restaurants.

I'm not claiming this kind of life is for everyone. Not at all. There is nothing wrong with a 9-5 job and life in the suburbs if that's what really resonates with you. There's nothing inherently noble about traveling or working some low wage odd job. The point is that it's too easy to choose things based on an artificially limited option set. It's too easy to define your life by stupid things like college majors or giant industry labels or titles that will make Aunt Bessie proud at the family reunion or salary levels.

The last one is especially dangerous.

It's a weird habit to measure your success in life only by the revenue side of the equation. Who cares if you bring in $100k a year if it only buys you a crappy apartment you hate in a city that stresses you out with friends that don't inspire you and a daily existence you mostly daydream about escaping from? Your costs exceed your revenues and you're actually going backward. You very well could get twice the lifestyle you desire at half the annual income. Like any business, the health of your personal life should be measured using both revenues and costs. On the personal level, neither are not just monetary.

Only you can know what kind of life you want. But getting off the conveyor belt of the education system, getting out of the home town expectations trap, and opening your mind to measures of progress beyond salary will give you a much better chance of crafting a life you love.

Begin with the End in Mind

I've never been really big on formal goals, goal setting, or visualization of a desired end-state. Instead, I focus on eliminating things I don't like and always making some kind of progress on things I do, even if towards a relatively open future. It's fun and mysterious.

But I've begun to realize something. Even though rarely formalized or deliberate, I've always dreamt and imagined myself and my projects in different future states. The more carefully I observe and recall, the more I see those imaginings becoming reality. It's subtle and sly sometimes, but it happens.

I am largely living a life I once imagined. I frequently have experiences where I'll stop and realize that what I just did is almost identical to something I dreamed up years before.

In recent years I've started getting a bit more deliberate with my visualizations of the future. I don't know what power, if any, it has to bring it about, but I have discovered the immense power such visualizing has to focus my mood and energy in the present. There's also the entertainment value of looking back on thought-out and written-out goals years later to see what I ended up creating and how well it tracked.

There is power in what we feed our subconscious mind. Power to push us forward or backward. Power to propel us toward a life we love, or to entrap us in a life we dread. It's largely a part of where we decide to channel our focus, and the stories we choose to tell ourselves.

I choose to begin with the end in mind. What do you choose to focus?

How to Discover What You Really Want? Don't.

What you really want to do with your life is a lot of things, many of which probably haven't been invented yet. How can you pick one and plot a path to it?

Instead, do the opposite. Think of things you know you hate doing or things that bore you or make you feel dead inside. Don't do those. Try new things and add to that list whenever you find something not for you. Make it your goal every day, week, month, and year to reduce the number of things you do that you don't like doing.

Don't think about careers, majors, titles, industries, and jobs. Think about activities. Stuff you do every day. What do you not want to do? How can you create a life where you never have to?

What you want is to not be bored in life. So find out what things you can quit, and find a way to quit doing them. Everything else is fair game.

That's always worked well for me anyway. Certainly better than trying to find out what I want to do.

Do What Works for You

Follow your passion, or follow your effort? Only go after what you love—your calling—or just knuckle down and get good at something? I think that's the wrong question.

It doesn't matter which side I fall on, or anyone else. It only matters what works for you. Both approaches are true. Who could disagree with trying to do something you love more than all your other options? Who could disagree that working hard and mastering something is more likely to bring you the things you want in life than half-assing it?

These approaches are both valid. They are both good advice.

Take the advice to follow your passion. The difficulty is that it's really, really hard work to find what you love. It's harder work to be honest about what you find. Harder still to do what it takes to achieve it.

Then take the advice to follow your effort. How do you choose where to put the effort? How do you know when the struggle will yield long-term benefit and when it's just useless suffering?

Both approaches still leave a lot of work to you. That's why it doesn't matter which you pick. When you hear someone giving one of these pieces of advice and you get excited and feel freed, that's the one for you. If you hear it and think it's a load of bullshit, that's not the one for you.

Go with the approach that resonates. Do whatever works for you.

Doing What You Love and Being Happy Are Not Necessarily the Same

Would you believe me if I told you that people can be happy doing work they hate?

Everyone wants to be happy. Well, there is actually some debate about what people want and whether the word "happy" is the most accurate. Call it utility, or fulfillment, or flow, or bliss, or the good life, or anything else you like. Consider use of the word 'happy' to describe an existence that maximizes those moments when you feel proud and thrilled to be alive, and minimizes those where you feel the opposite.

Most people also think they want to do work that they love. That is, they want the way in which they procure the resources needed for survival and material pleasure to be an activity inherently interesting and fulfilling. They do not merely want the hunt to be done for the meat, but they want to enjoy it for its own pleasures. At least that's what they'll tell you.

You might be lying.

I think a great many people are lying to themselves and others about what they actually want. A lot of people want to be the type of person who seeks meaning in their work, but they actually care a lot more about finding a way to get the resources needed just to relax more. Doing work you love is harder than doing work you can tolerate. It's not a bad thing. There is nothing morally superior or inherently noble about wanting to do work that you love, and there is nothing bad about wanting to just get the money you need to work as little as possible. These are personal preferences, and either approach can lead to a happy life. Of course, lack of self-knowledge or dishonesty with oneself about which approach you prefer can lead to unhappiness just as easily.

In other words, doing work you love is not the secret ingredient needed to be happy. At least not for everyone.

There are people who can never be happy unless they are doing work they love. For them, it doesn't even matter if they make a lot of money at it. If those people chase money and status over fulfilling work, they'll be miserable.

There are also people who can never be happy unless they have a large amount of money, free time, leisure, and a minimum of stress. For them, it doesn't even matter much what kind of work they do, as long as it yields them enough money in a small enough amount of time to do what they really love. If those people chase a meaningful career with all the material and time sacrifices that requires, they'll be miserable.

Who are you?

The key to happiness is to discover which type of person you are, be honest with yourself and others about what you find, and have the courage to live it. Let's illustrate this with a matrix.

Doing Work You Love

	Yes	No
Happy Yes	Passionate Founder Blissful Ski Instructor	4 Hour Work Weeker Deferred Gratification Grinder
Happy No	Envious Artist Angry Adjunct	Soul-Dead 9-5er Lifestyle Slave

Let's walk through each of the four quadrants one by one. See if you can recognize people in your life who fit them.

Oh, and notice in particular the fact that the amount of money earned is not the relevant factor in any of the quadrants. You can have rich, poor, or anything in between in any of them.

"I love my work and I'm happy"

The upper left quadrant represents those people who have gone all-in to find work that makes them feel alive every day. They may be billionaire tech company founders who live and breath their company, or penniless beach bums who spend all day on the waves and scrape together just enough money giving lessons for a burger and a brew. I know people so passionately obsessed with their work that they'd rather be doing it than anything else. Depending upon what that work is, they may be very wealthy or very poor. They don't much care. They care about their craft, and so long as they're doing it, life is good.

"I hate my work and I'm happy"

The upper right quadrant is where people who have accepted the fact that work is not for them hang out. They've also come to grips with the fact that the things they actually do love require a good bit of money and time, and work is required to get it. They configure their lives to do the minimum amount of drudgery to get the maximum payoff. I know business owners who have no interest in their industry, or salespeople who would just as unhappily sell something totally different. They just found a niche where they can get what they need.

They sometimes live the *Four Hour Workweek* life, and truly put in almost no time to keep the income stream going. Those with a longer time horizon and ability to defer gratification may put in a lot more hours upfront and endure a high degree of boredom for the payoff of evenings, weekends, or retirement. I know people who I don't think would ever find happiness in any kind of work. They want leisure. But they've made their peace with this fact and put all their energy into being true to that reality, instead of unhappily chasing an illusive form of work they'd love, or feeling guilty for their material desires.

"I love my work and I'm unhappy"

Consider the martyr. The people in the lower left quadrant are probably the hardest for me to be around. They self-righteously remind everyone about how they opted not to "sell-out", but then never stop bitching about the costs they incurred for doing so. The truth is these are people who would be happier seeking money instead of work they think the world will see as meaningful. This is the jazz artist who gets angry every time the Grammy's come along and some blonde pop star takes home the hardware. This is the adjunct professor who chose an obscure academic discipline with almost no chance of good money but never stops yelling about the injustice in the fact that no one values what they do enough to pay them big bucks. The funny thing is, this is a phenomenon found almost exclusively in rich countries. The unhappy work purists are typically quite wealthy by world standards, but they can never stop comparing themselves to the richest of the rich. This obsessive tendency to compare reveals their true preference for material wealth over career fulfillment. They'd be a lot happier if they were simply honest with themselves and, as my friend Jason Brennan suggests, got a job at Geico.

"I hate my work and I'm unhappy"

Opposite of the previous category, those in the lower right quadrant believe themselves to be made happiest by money, status, and "normalcy". But they are wrong about their true desires. These people chose the best school, the best major, the best internship, and the job with the best title at the consulting firm because everyone around them egged them on the whole way. Surely a great job, nice house, respectable resume, and good income will lead to happiness, right? In their case, wrong.

They find themselves hating their work and not really enjoying the material benefits it brings either. Their weekends are just as dull as the workweek. As they keep ratcheting up the career ladder they also ratchet up their lifestyle, hoping that the next level and a new car will bring happiness. It doesn't. But because their material quality of life escalates with their income, they feel trapped. If they happen to realize that they never cared much for money and status as much as meaning in their work, it seems too late. How could they give up $180,000 a year to start a band or become a chef? They might lose their marriage, and surely their social standing.

Knowledge and honesty

Again, every quadrant has examples of both rich and poor within it. The two happy categories include rich and poor as well as those who love their work and those who hate it. The key is not finding the one true path that works for everyone. The key is finding out who you really are. Then not being ashamed of what you find and not lying to yourself about it.

Self-knowledge and self-honesty

Finally, after discovering and being truthful about what makes you happy, go do it. It's worth all the costs.

Hedonism as Life Purpose

A theologian named John Piper coined the phrase "Christian Hedonism," ascribing the chief end of man being *"to glorify God by enjoying Him forever."* Whether or not you are religious there's something powerful in it.

As revealed by the book, Piper proposes the Christian's purpose in life is to take delight in existence, and take delight in God delighting in them for being delighted. God created humans so that he could take pleasure in them, and seeing man take pleasure in life is what most pleased God.

I always associated the idea with a line from the movie Chariots of Fire, where the deeply religious Eric Liddell is chastised by his sister for missing church because he was running. He said, *"When I run I feel His pleasure."* Not merely that Liddell was having a pleasurable experience himself, but that he felt the pleasure of God as he ran.

C.S. Lewis's book, *The Four Loves,* describes the deep love that occurs when people are not only delighting in each other, but delighting that the other is delighting in them.

The word hedonism evokes excess, even destructive excess. That's a very shallow understanding of the idea. It is true if one merely indulges in short-run highs they may be considered a hedonist. But I believe genuine hedonism, as the satisfaction of desires, is in fact life's purpose. The trick is discovering what those desires are and what it takes to satisfy them. Running is not easy the way drinking a beer is easy. Running is hard and at least a bit painful. Yet Liddell described a kind of pleasure that far exceeds a mere exciting of the taste buds.

The deepest, truest human desires are not satisfied with temporary titillation alone. Those can be a delightful part of existence, but cannot satisfy the soul's most powerful longings. Being fully alive requires some degree of challenge. It requires some degree of pushing oneself, if even only to fight distraction and carve out time to marvel or think.

That is not to say it is only found in quiet contemplation. Many of life's most fulfilling moments are busy, bustling, social affairs. But it seems true delight is best derived when some effort is required to obtain it. It requires both connection to self and connection to something outside of oneself. Simply taking what the stream of life floats us can be a decent indulgence, but it slowly erodes or numbs a deeper sense of meaning.

Hedonism as a conscious pursuit isn't easy. The self-knowledge and self-honesty required to take genuine delight in existence, and feel a kind of reciprocal delight being taken in you–whether by another, or by God, or by the universe, or whatever you may call it–is hard won. It's easier to let life happen to you and play the critic or the martyr.

With or without a religious narrative, the notion of finding your highest pleasure and pursuing it is powerful. That seemingly paradoxical combination of the words, "Christian", and, "Hedonist" has wisdom in it. The former carries connotations of discipline, devotion, and the eschewing of worldly distractions. The latter connotes joy, pleasure, and seizing every moment for pure delight. That combination seems to be where the best life is found.

Perhaps the pursuit of pleasure is in fact a serious affair; as serious as life itself.

Joy and the Other

One of the key elements of living a life of joy is the idea of a kind of reciprocity of delight. Fulfillment seems to require more than delight for one self, but some other in which to delight and be delighted. As adventurer Chris McCandless scribbled in the final weeks of his life, *"Happiness only real when shared."* To become your true self as an individual requires some other to be differentiated from, to collaborate with, and to enjoy.

However, that Other need not be only human. There is a sense in which the ultimate Other is something far broader and greater than any one person. When you feel like the world itself is collaborating with you, that is when you feel true joy. Seeing reality as something not in opposition to you, but working with you. The religious might call it divine will. The mystics might call it their Muse. The non-religious might consider it living in line with the laws of the universe. Astrologer Rob Brezsny calls it pronoia, "The suspicion that the Universe is a conspiracy on your behalf." Whatever it might be, there's a powerful analogy in the thought.

Consider acts of creation. Painting, storytelling, songwriting, and the like. There is a meaningful sense in which, in a state of flow, more is going on than just the creator producing. The page gives back. You develop a theme and play it and the music doesn't just come from you, it gets right back in you and inspires you even as it is inspired by you. If you give yourself to the art fully it gives something back to you. In a romantic relationship the same effect is at work. Being in love requires more than just admiration of another. Your feelings are enhanced by the knowledge and evidence that you are adored in return.

This need for an Other in order to experience joy is radically individualistic. It's the opposite of an absorption of unique individuals into a universal blob. In order to experience this reciprocal relationship with reality we have to get to know our unique selves. We must be so differentiated that we cannot mistake anything or anyone else's purposes for our own. Then we can fully experience the joy of our own purpose by interacting harmoniously with others.

The Neutrality of Everything

A hammer is neither good nor bad. It is a tool. It is useful. It can be useful in achieving good things, and equally useful in achieving bad things. It is valuable because it is useful, but the fact that it has value does not make it good or bad.

The same is true of an iPhone. The same is true of money. These are all morally neutral, inanimate objects (Siri notwithstanding) that become extensions of human will and volition, and act as a catalyst for whatever good or bad ends we intend. They deserve neither vilification nor praise, except in regards to their usefulness.

Tools have their own qualities and characteristics; they have their own nature. They will react in certain ways to certain conditions. If you slam an iPhone down on a hard surface, it will crack. It's silly to get angry at the characteristics of the iPhone. Part of growing up is learning to understand and work with the natures of the objects around us, rather than being surprised or angered by them.

So much for tools. What about people? Immanuel Kant, along with just about every decent person I've met, would bristle at the thought of people as morally neutral tools; useful if properly employed, but neither praise nor blameworthy in and of themselves. For good reason. People as objects is probably a terrible and incorrect notion. People have wills and can choose right or wrong. People don't just react. They can act to thwart one another. They have qualities that take them beyond the level of tools. That may be their place in the cosmos, but what about in our day-to-day perceptions?

It can be incredibly enlightening and freeing to treat people with the same neutrality we treat our iPhones. Not because they are the same, but because seeing them that way can help shed bitterness and accomplish more. If, just like you would with an inanimate object, we try to learn the natures of those around us and get an idea of how they will react to conditions around them, we will be better equipped to cooperate for mutual benefit.

Sure, they have motives, but ascribing motives and assuming intentions are often hindrances to productive relationships. Whether or not it's for good reason, if you know a person gets angry every time you say X, rather than begrudge them this habit, adapt. Learn to navigate the world of human relationships with the same judgment-free attitude you do the non-human world. People have natures. They'll act in accordance with them. Don't hold it against them. Instead, learn it, know it, expect it, and work with it.

There are certainly times when some kind of confrontation or intervention is required. There are times when working around a person's modus operandi may be worse than trying to help them see the need to change it. Yet these times are mostly rare, and only really worth it when a kind of standing invitation to do so exists in the relationship.

See how it works to view people as morally neutral, rational agents, rather than out to help or harm you. It can turn even unpleasant interactions into a kind of interesting puzzle. It may be untrue, but it is useful and, in some ways, makes it easier to appreciate people and treat them well.

Life as a Game

The great storyteller C.S. Lewis says in one of his stories that some of the most sinister things are those that look like or pretend to be something they are not. I'd modify this slightly and say that the worst things are those that actually believe themselves to be something they are not. Life is full of stories and games. It is not the playing or telling that causes trouble, but when we begin to believe the game is the reality.

Take sports. Imagine if a professional football player actually believed that the game was life. If winning was not just the artificial end within the construct of the game, but the actual end in life, you might see things like the scene in the ridiculous movie *Any Given Sunday*, where a player shoots a would be tackler. Players would hurt or kill opponents regularly and some would proudly become martyrs just to win.

Critics of sports will say that this already occurs, but if you think hard about it, even the most over-committed behave as if they are in a game and that life is something else. The most criticized decisions, like bounties for injuring players, or keeping an injured player in, are egregious precisely because it is so universally acknowledged that sports is a game and it is improper to treat it like life.

It's harder to see the other games and stories, and games and stories nested within games and stories, that we regularly engage in. Language itself is a kind of game. When you transform an idea into a mental image or words in your mind, you produce a symbol that represents the idea, but not perfectly.

When you put those symbols into audible form, they are still less representative of the core idea. The hearer unbundles the words and facial expressions, translates them into ideas in their own mind, and finally translates them into a response or action. At the end of this game, the action of the hearer may manifest something quite different from the idea with which you began. You played the game of verbal communication. The better you are at the game, the better you become at achieving your desired response.

But this paints too simple a picture of the games we play. Language takes place in a social context, nested within several overlapping games. If you are talking at a work party, everyone involved is operating within a rich narrative about appropriate behavior, what words and actions mean, who relates to who in what ways, who plays what roles within the group, and so on. We are regularly navigating multiple complex narratives and games.

This is not a bad thing. Games and stories are useful and inevitable. We haven't yet found a way to telepathically share abstract ideas, and I'm not even sure we'd enjoy it if we could. Games and stories help us make sense of the world, form relationships, predict causality, and move closer to our goals. Games are useful and they're also a lot of fun. The danger is when you forget it's a game and think it's life itself.

I hate formal attire. It's uncomfortable and I think it looks like a silly costume. Still, in certain contexts, a game has evolved wherein everyone wears certain costumes that come bundled with certain signals and ideas. I play the game, even if I sometimes wish everyone would find a more comfortable way to create the context of formality. I don't mistake the game for real life–and thank goodness. If being a savvy dresser was the goal; if it was itself success, seriousness, intelligence; I'd be in trouble. I'm not very good at dressing well. Luckily, it's a game and a way to communicate these concepts, albeit imperfectly, and it is tied up with a lot of other ways to communicate. I can do it enough to get by, but if dressing well meant living well, I'd be having a rough go of life. By recognizing unspoken dress codes as a game, I can actually have some fun with them and not feel so choked by my necktie.

Upon seeing games for what they are, it's tempting to refuse to play and reject them altogether in favor of *"the real thing"*. This is a mistake in the opposite direction. There may be a time when I can always refuse to wear a suit and it won't harm me, but for now, it would hinder my other goals in life. It would alienate me from people whose company I enjoy. I try not to be bitter at the games people play, but enter in on my own terms and navigate them toward my own ends.

Even a hermit monk plays games. He has entered a narrative that gives explanatory power to his unusual behavior, and thereby protects him from some of the hurt that comes from not being understood. The social story of the hermit exists as a kind of fortress within which he can opt-out of other games with less harm to his relationships with others.

It is incredibly liberating to realize the game-like nature of life. We are constantly telling and acting in stories and playing games. Once we awaken to this realization, we can step back and remind ourselves that the object of the particular game ought not be confused with the object of our life.

We can seek to find the truth that resonates with us to our core, but on our journey we will inevitably have to play games with their own objectives. Don't despise or run away from the games, but don't forget that they're just games!

Play them, enjoy them, master them, fail at them, laugh at them, love them. It will make your journey towards fulfillment a better one.

Age and Your Option Set

A lot of young people possess the skills, interest, maturity, and resources to do right now the very thing they want to be doing in five years. Sadly, almost none of them realize it or feel free to do it now. They feel as though they need permission, or need to be in the "normal" age bracket for it to be in their set of options.

I know some coders who have the skill and interest to work for a software startup. They don't enjoy school. They don't feel it's making them a better coder. They have a job offer right now to go work someplace they love. They even say that the job offer is exactly the kind they want to get in four years when they finish school, and voice disappointment that it came their way too early. How could it be too early? The company wants you and you want them, right now, today!

The conveyor belt mindset is so strong in most of us that we are incapable of seeing options in front of us if they aren't part of the set of options that is supposed to be in front of a 16, 18, or 24 year old. At 18 your options are among different colleges, internships, summer jobs, or gap year programs. That's the norm, and that norm blinds people to the massively larger set of options they actually have. This blinding is so strong that even when offered something that they hope will be available four years hence, they are unable to see it as a serious, viable option, and they say no to go

...through something less interesting for four years and ...ld thousands.

This isn't just about college. Our tendency to stick with the age-defined conveyor belt option set society expects is strong throughout life. I've met women who desperately want to stop working to have and raise children, but they feel like they aren't allowed to until they've put in a certain amount of time as a workingwoman, even though they could afford it today. I've met people who want to play gigs at bars with a band, but they feel that's the kind of thing an accountant can only do when he retires.

Don't be blinded by social averages and expectations. If you want to learn code today, who cares that you're only 10 and supposed to be doing other things. If you want to switch careers, who cares that you're 60 and it's supposed to be too late for that. If you have a job offer today that matches what you hope to get after graduation, who cares if you're only 18.

The conveyor belt sucks. Get off. Pave your own path.

Lack of patience can cripple us,

Your Lack of Income Can Be an Asset

Let's say you want to do something awesome. Maybe you're interested in being a part of a startup or an entrepreneurial business. Maybe you've got a creative side, and you'd jump at the chance to work on a movie script. The less cushy your current life, the higher the chance you'll be in a position to answer when opportunity knocks. The lower the cost of exit, the easier exit becomes.

A lot of young people just starting out in their careers feel pressure to scratch and claw for a few thousand more in salary and keep up with friends who are moving into nicer houses, driving nicer cars, eating sushi every Tuesday, and shopping at trendy places. There's nothing wrong with any of these things, but if you have a stomach for more risk than the average person, and a desire to do some really cool stuff, you might want to resist the urge to upgrade your lifestyle. Your relatively low income can be a huge asset.

Even the most frugal and self-controlled among us have a propensity to adopt a standard of living right up to our capacity (sometimes beyond). It makes sense. In fact, it'd be a little weird if you were raking in cash and sleeping on a park bench, just waiting for the opportunity to use your capital. Living in the moment is fine. The thing is, there are so many ways to happily do this. I've found that, whatever the income level, once it's above a certain very low baseline, you can organize a pretty happy life around it. The higher it goes, the more you spend and it is damn-near impossible to go backwards.

I knew a guy once who had a great job, making more than any of his peers, but at a place that pressured employees to upgrade their cars, houses, etc. He soon found himself in a lifestyle only that well-paid job could sustain. Then the job turned sour. He wanted out. But how to convince his wife, his kids, and himself to downgrade the car, the monthly budget, the mortgage? Some of these things couldn't be done at all on short notice. His high income was not a source of freedom, but a chain, preventing him from doing what he wanted.

So you're young and your income is low. That's a huge advantage for you. That means if your friend tells you she wants you to help launch a new business, but you might not get paid for the first six months, you can probably swing it, since you're already accustomed to eating Ramen and you have no DirecTV to cancel. Some of the best and brightest are incapable of jumping on great opportunities because they've earned decent money quickly, then hemmed themselves in, unable to ever downgrade their short term quality of life. If you can, you have a competitive edge.

Obviously, no one wants to stay forever on a diet of canned chicken. But when you're young, and at the beginning of the discovery process of what makes you come alive, it's helpful to be free from a huge list of material needs. You'd be surprised how much an early high income can stall further progress towards your goals.

So if you think you're poor compared to your friends, smile.

When you consider all your assets and liabilities—your skills, interests, strengths, weaknesses, capital, time, flexibility, etc.— include on the asset side of the ledger the fact that you don't really need much money to maintain your current quality of life. It may come in handy when the chance to do something amazing, and far more rewarding in the long term (materially and otherwise), emerges and you're ready to jump while your buddies have to turn it down to stay with a job that pays for their $15 "happy hour" cocktails.

Waging Generational Warfare Against Yourself

There's a wonderful book called *How They Succeeded* that highlights the paths of a few individuals most would consider to be successful by all of today's standards. What struck me was how many of the highly accomplished individuals interviewed mentioned staying out of debt as a key to success. It's obvious that being debt free has practical benefits like the ability to accumulate capital, the maintenance of good credit, and a good reputation. But these seemed rather simple, obvious, and not enough to warrant the repeated advice. None of them mentioned personal hygiene or other obvious practical disciplines, so why debt?

There are reasons beyond the practical and material for minimizing debt. There is a psychological loss of freedom that can take place with the knowledge of debt hanging over one's head. This can subtly subvert freethinking and creativity and narrow the lens through which one sees the world.

This is probably not the case for everyone in every circumstance. If you're involved in lots of business endeavors where you need to operate on credit, you may be very comfortable with and adept at handling debt. I know people who do not seem to have any trouble with a constantly fluctuating personal balance sheet. It's not that way for me. I definitely feel the steady pressure of debt like white noise in the background of all I do.

On the one hand, it seems odd that debt would be problematic. Borrowing money from the probable excess of the future to subsidize consumption of the tighter present can make financial sense and result in an overall increase in enjoyment of life. Indeed, if we never changed or grew and our preferences were the same through time, debt would make perfect sense as a way to smooth the ups and downs of material pleasures. But that's just it; we change.

Debt often has the unfortunate side effect of handcuffing us to decisions we made as a younger, less wise version of ourselves. For instance, if you were determined to be a lawyer or a doctor at a young age and persisted down that path and realized you no longer enjoyed it, your options may have narrowed with your skill set.

In such a state, we become captives to the choices of an earlier self. It's no different with consumption decisions than educational or career decisions. Going in to debt is a way for your present self to borrow from your future self. Think about the level of presumption. Are you really confident your future self will be the type of person who would think it a good idea? Might future you have other uses to put the debt payments to?

When you go into debt, you are binding another person – your future self – to subsidize the desires of your present self. It may be a good idea in some cases, but it warrants very careful consideration. It's not merely a question of whether your future self will have the resources to subsidize your present preferences; it's also a question of whether you'll be happy about doing it.

I don't want to be bitter at my former self for the financial obligations I have. I'd rather the self of the past, present, and future work together towards the fulfillment of our individual and shared life goals.

Debt Will Limit Your Options

It's hard to find a way to combine your career with your passion. It's much harder if you need to make a lot of money to pay for your lifestyle, loans, etc. I know a number of people who make lots of money–enough to make that law degree a sound financial investment, for example–but hate what they do. The sound financial investment–trading debt for a ticket to a high paying job–turns out to have limited their options to only jobs that pay well enough to service the debt, and they ended up not liking those jobs.

In other words, the lower your wage requirements, the more flexibility you have early on to explore and test and find work you love. Keep that in mind with each step. Ask whether your present decisions are limiting your future options in a way you might regret.

I don't mean to pick on law students with the above example, but that's the one I see the most. People get a law degree because they're smart, and they imagine a law degree as opening up a lot of career options. But, after they graduate and have huge debts to pay, the number of jobs that cover it are limited. If you don't enjoy corporate law, you might feel trapped.

It's not just education debt that can limit you to jobs you don't like. I've also met a lot of people who feel stuck with a high paying job they hate because they bought an expensive house or car. If a nicer house and a less enjoyable job is a trade-off you're happy with, by all means go for it! But it's hard to undo once you jump in, so be cautious and thoughtful.

Normal is Overrated

I think most people don't do most things to feel excited, or safe, or happy. I think most people do most things to feel normal.

We have this bizarre, powerful urge to behave similar to those around us. If we live around farmers, farming is normal. If we live among intellectuals, reading is normal. If we live in a world where 16 year olds go to high school and 20 year olds go to college, those are the normal things to do.

The worst crime is to be abnormal. It's worse than being unhappy or depressed. If you're depressed in your normal station in life–age 35, married, one kid, a finance job at $70k a year, a two bedroom house, and a dog–no one will really care that much. They will feel unthreatened by you. Sure, they'll want you to be happy, but not as much as they want you to be normal.

If you were to be ridiculously happy, but highly abnormal–age 35, married and 13 kids. Or age 35, no permanent residence, vagabonding the world. Or age 35, a new startup every six months and a love of dancing in public–people, probably including your parents, would be far more troubled than if you were normal and depressed. Being abnormal forces others to confront their own normalcy, and few things are more frightening.

The urge to be normal is the driving force behind most people's educational choices, career choices, consumer choices, and even relationship choices. But normal is overrated, and sometimes arbitrary or even counter to your individual nature.

I don't think deliberate attempts to be abnormal are any kind of solution. Nor do I think there is no logic behind this drive toward normalcy. If you want to make friends and communicate with people, some level of shared experience is necessary.

Conventions emerge for a reason. The problem is, we often stop asking why a particular desire or convention is beneficial, and we just assume it is because it's common. What's common is often exactly the wrong thing for you, because you are by definition not common. You are you, and there is only one.

A good test to see whether or not you are doing what you do to be normal, rather than to achieve your own best living experience, is to listen to the words you use.

When asked why you do something you don't enjoy if you find the words, "Because I have to" on your lips, that's the normalcy urge talking.

You don't have to do anything just because people would think it weird if you didn't.

Just be you.

☆ pay attention

Gains from a Radically Different Daily Structure

Have you ever stood in a fast-food restaurant around noon on a weekday, with the line almost out the door? Or made your daily commute during the rush-hour traffic?

Why should we all wait so long to get food when an hour or two later the cooks and servers would be waiting around with few customers? Why should we all sit in bumper-to-bumper traffic expanding 15-minute drives into hours of unpleasant honking?

The same is true for holiday shopping, parking on the weekends, and prices during vacation. The absurdity of the suffering we all endure and the economic and psychic cost of all this waiting, planning, and crowding is hard to measure. But it's real.

It all stems from the same source: the regimentation of life. Every kid goes to school at the exact same time every day, stays for the same number of hours, leaves at the same time, and has the same days off. More variation exists in the working world, but not much. The bulk of producers clock in at roughly the same time every morning, eat lunch in unison, and head home en masse.

The odd thing is none of this is necessary for a growing number, possibly even most of us. How many jobs require someone to actually be physically present between the hours of 9 and 5? Why the heck do kids need to sit in clumps of same aged children for identical hours to be forced to study the same things in the same way?

We can work from almost anywhere. We can learn from almost anywhere. Most of us have the tools, the freedom of movement, and the resources. Why don't we see a diversity of daily schedules? Why don't more people treat Tuesday as the weekend? Why don't more people do all their errands during the day and their work at night? Why don't more people abandon regular offices or classrooms altogether?

There are some benefits of the regimen, but not enough to justify the costs we endure. These practices continue primarily because of a mindset. We have status quo bias. We feel guilt or confusion at the idea of not being present 9-5 at work or 8-3 at school. It's an obsession with externally defined roles and goals at the expense of outcomes and value created.

What do we want and need to learn or create or earn? How and when can we best do it? Those are the important questions and the answers, if we are honest, would vary widely and look little like the routines most of us subject ourselves to.

Imagine a world where kids freely explored, worked, played, and learned on their own terms and timelines. Imagine a world where people of all ages worked when and how they worked best. Imagine a week not punctuated by any regular rush hour or weekend or mealtime.

Certainly patterns would emerge and some schedules would be more common than others, but absent our rigid adherence to an outdated schedule, supply and demand would be regulated by the money, time, and headache of peaks and troughs, and the market would smooth out and have smaller ups and downs.

The value of such a shift would be immense. Think of how many hours people would not be sitting in traffic if few had to show up at the same time to the office or school in the morning. Think about the hours and money that would not be spent during peak times for flights, hotels, parking lots, and Disney World tickets.

Think of the immense subjective value enhancement by not enduring the throngs. Little if any of these major gains would show up in GDP measurements. In fact, it may hurt GDP. Less spending on the same goods. Less need for parking structures, etc.

We are seeing a slow but steady move in this direction, which is part of the reason I've argued that GDP is a dated and increasingly useless measure of anything valuable. Let's speed up the process by asking "*Why not?*" instead of "*Why?*" about radical new structures that make us happier.

You let your kids unschool? Why not?

You work remotely? Why not?

You take the day off to go to the beach in the middle of the day? Why not?

It might not be doable for you in any big ways, but I bet there are some stressful patterns in your life that are relics of a bygone era and can be shed with little difficulty.

What are you waiting for?

Against Life Plans

Life plans seem pretty daunting to me. I know people who feel stressed and depressed because they don't have a clear one. There are incredibly rare people who know beyond the shadow of a doubt what they want to do in great detail. If you are one of them, don't let anything stop you. For the rest of us, I suggest we drop the notion of a life plan altogether.

Trying to find what you love is not the best idea. How can you know with so many options? It might not even exist yet. Instead, make a list of what you know you don't like. Don't do those things, and everything else is fair game and moving you closer to the things you love.

But it's not just about narrowing down and finding the things you most enjoy. It's about enjoying the process. Try a bunch of stuff. Don't waste time once you know for sure something makes you unhappy. Not only do you want to drop it because it's not likely to be your long term sweet spot, but also because it's not fulfilling right now.

Every day do your best to avoid things that truly make you unhappy and crush your spirit. Every day show up, create, work, and do things that are fulfilling, even if (especially if) they are really hard work.

You don't have to plan your life, but you should live it. Fully alive. Fully awake.

If you're not in a spot where you're enjoying life right now, why not? Can you change it? Not two or ten years from now, but today.

Every day get a little bit closer to only doing things you really enjoy. You'll end up with a life better than what you would plan if you could.

Forget about Long-Term Strategic Planning

We serious adult types really value planning and prepping and researching and approaching problems in a well-considered manner. We also overestimate our own ability to plan and predict the future, and our efforts to do so can be a big hindrance on living a good life.

When you're thinking not just of the next move, but a long sequence of moves and counter moves based on the probability of how others will respond, you get into some pretty dicey territory. If you are an expert chess player, this is exactly how you want to play (or so I've heard). It works because chess is bounded. There are only so many moves, and when you've mastered the game you can quickly narrow down the variables and predict the set of options several moves out. The squares, pieces, and rules of movement are the same, move after move, game after game.

Imagine a chessboard that, as you were pondering and planning a long sequence of moves, changed shape? Then a third player joined with her own pieces, and those pieces didn't move by the same rules. Then the pieces started talking to each other and your Rook quit and joined the white Queen to form an independent alliance. Then the black Pawns invented machine guns...you get the point. This is more like life. There are way too many variables and complexities to plan many steps ahead.

There are some big benefits to taking a more modest approach. I was recently reminded of a great TED talk about the spaghetti and marshmallow tower challenge. Teams are given some sticks of dry pasta, a bit of tape and string, and a marshmallow and have a time limit within which to build the tallest tower with a marshmallow on top. Apparently, MBA's are pretty bad at the challenge, and little kids are pretty good at it.

The MBA's spend all their time working on the single perfect plan, then build it and place the marshmallow on top just as time expires. Then it collapses. They have so much discussion and prep and detailed delegation of tasks that the plan becomes very rigid, and every single part has to work perfectly or the whole thing will (literally) crumble.

The kids take a different approach. They just started building immediately. They throw together small structures and put the marshmallow on top. Then they take it apart and make a bigger one. They rapidly prototype. They just start learning about the pieces and possibilities in front of them by directly engaging with them. They plan no further than the first idea that comes to mind.

I once heard a podcaster say she always loses to her young daughter in Jenga for the same reason. She's so focused on the position of the blocks five moves from now that she doesn't always make the best decision in the moment. Her daughter keeps it simple and lives in the moment, always plucking the safest possible piece on every turn.

That's how I manage to survive playing tennis with my wife, who actually knows how to play the game. I know I lack the

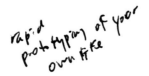

rapid prototyping of your own life

technique and strategy she has, so I simply go all out to return every shot and just keep it in play. I figure at some point she'll make a mistake. Plus, when I try to get tricky and set up a sequence of shots, it usually goes wrong.

There is overlooked value in the novice approach. Just taking in the resources currently before you and fully diving in to the problem at hand has major advantages over long deliberation and planning. When you're a kid or a novice with nothing to lose, why not take a stab?

We may gain expertise in many things and develop the ability to plan into the future with greater detail, but we shouldn't mistake expertise at a single thing like chess or tennis for expertise at life.

In life, we are all novices. We've never (as far as we know) lived before, and we have no idea what will happen at any moment. The way you might plan a single, solitary event like the construction of a house (if you've ever done that, you know that never goes as planned either!) doesn't translate to the span of your life.

Take some pressure off of yourself and don't stress about what Job A or School B next fall will mean for your retirement account 40 years down the road. You have no idea. No one does.

Take stock of your loves and hates, do more of the former and less of the latter, and seize on the best opportunities before you. If it's not working, take a lesson from the prototyping kids. Adapt, grab the sticks, and try a different approach.

Obsessed with Options, Blind to Opportunities

One of the first steps in your personal emancipation is to realize that the world is full of options, and the few things currently in front of you are not the only from which to choose. But there is a difference between options and opportunities.

Options are theoretical. Opportunities are actual. Options are statistical probabilities. Opportunities are singular, concrete instances. Options can always be added on, and the option set can always grow as an aggregate bundle, so there is no urgency or scarcity in options. Opportunities are temporary and cannot be aggregated. Each is too unique and cannot be replicated.

The finite nature of each individual opportunity can be scary. It feels more comforting to stay in the abstract world of options than to jump in to a real opportunity, which immediately reduces the set of theoretical other options.

Options thinking can be useful to gain some big picture long-term perspective, but it's a dangerous mindset too because it can blind you to opportunities or limit the ways you can gain from them. Here are three of the downsides to thinking about options instead of opportunities.

Too Good for That

Because options are a giant aggregate of all possible activities, the field will always look better than a specific, individual opportunity. When you know that the field is available to you, real actions always seem a little less glamorous. The problem is that the field is not available to you.

Your life isn't like gambling. You can't pick the field. You have to settle on specific actions. Grumpiness can result when you do specific things but obsess about keeping your options open. You'll always think you're too good for whatever you're doing and never fully throw yourself behind it. This will, paradoxically, further limit your options as those around you will tire of your attitude of superiority and belief that, if you wanted to, you could be doing something better. It keeps you from entering in to the moment and doing your best work.

Myth of the Perfect Path

The purpose of options is to be able to choose one or more at some point. But, after spending a lot of time expanding your theoretical option set towards this end, pressure can begin to build. When you finally do choose something specific, you'd better get it right. Options thinking can make you so aware of opportunity cost of foregone activities that it puts an unbearable burden on whatever you do choose to be perfect. This short-circuits the best of all human learning techniques: trial and error. No trial occurs when error is so feared.

The endless keeping of options open in search for the perfect assumes too much about your ability to know all variables–including your own changing desires and interests–and deprives you of one of the best discovery tools: failure. All this stress about choosing the mythical one true path leads to another problem.

Paralysis by Analysis

The ceaseless break-down comparisons, the cost-benefit analyses, the consideration of these seemingly weighty matters can itself become an activity so consuming it prevents you from all others. You can become bogged down in a quagmire of strategic planning and never take the definite actions necessary to achieve anything.

The real problem is that inaction is also an action. Not choosing is a choice. Waiting, watching, thinking on the sidelines has a cost that's even higher than the cost of choosing an imperfect opportunity. When you take opportunity B it means you can no longer take A or C. That's the cost. But the benefit is you get whatever goodness is to be had from B, and the self-knowledge of how well B suits you. Even if you fail at it you gain something. When you get stuck analyzing all three options you not only miss out on A and C, but you forgo the benefits of B as well.

Expanding your options set can be intoxicating. For a time, it feels so fast paced and exciting. I could do anything! Why would I do this one thing when I could keep entertaining all the possible things I could do in my mind?

It's all right to play with your options and expand them and think about them from time to time. But you've got to put options in their place as subordinate statistical playthings when compared to opportunities.

Options don't change the world or the holder of them. Actions do.

Success as a Discipline

I like to view success as a skill not unlike any other. Something that can be learned. If you apply discipline and form good habits you will get better at success.

Perhaps there are elements of heredity or good fortune that might bring a person success or the appearance of it. But those are less common and tend to be fleeting. In fact, if you have not learned success as a discipline, even good fortune could end up making you worse off in the long run.

Success is the ability to imagine a desired end and achieve it. Both components–the imagining and the achieving–are important. The thing that connects them and ties ideas to outcomes is a willingness to pay the price. Many people imagine lovely things and get upset or confused when they don't get them. But few are realistic about whether or not they actually are willing to do what it takes.

How can you learn the discipline of success? You learn by doing.

First imagine something you want. Then think through what it will take to achieve it. Decide if you're willing to pay the price and if so, fully commit. Now begin taking the steps and don't stop until you achieve it. That's it. Each time you accomplish what you set out to, you begin to form a habit and become accustomed to the process of success. For this reason, as with any other skill, start small.

Think of modest goals and ends that aren't too far off. Practice achieving them and you not only get whatever the end was, but you learn how to succeed. Do it over and over. Once you've mastered success as a discipline, you can apply it to more grand and ambitious ends.

I don't mean to imply that you can succeed every time you try anything. Skills don't work that way.

You can't master piano playing such that you'll never make a mistake and you can play anything perfectly the first time. But we all recognize piano playing as a skill that can be cultivated through discipline and the formation of habits.

Success is the same. You can teach yourself how to imagine a goal, commit to paying the price, and reach it.

The Expedition of Our Age

Nothing is guaranteed. There is no plan or path that can ensure the kind of life you want. There are only opportunities with varying degrees of risk. Sometimes the least risky opportunities are also those least likely to result in fulfillment. The great success stories are the result of daring expedition and pursuit of unique goals.

There was a time when a college education was something of an adventure. It was exclusive, not easy to get, and signaled something special. Leaving your hometown for a university was a big deal, a great expedition. This is no longer true.

Going to college is not difficult today. It's not elite or rare. Most young people can easily travel and live away from their hometowns and many have even before college. Today, college isn't much of an adventure. In fact, it attracts some of the most risk averse individuals, and, perhaps paradoxically, the higher ranked the school often the more risk averse its students.

There is a small but growing number of young people who see this and they've got the itch. They go to college only to realize it's a warmed over version of all the years of safe, institutional schooling they've just completed. No one will question their decision to go. No one will call them crazy. The risk of flunking out is as minuscule as the risk of standing out. The sense of adventure is gone, replaced with a sense of perpetual adolescence and paternalistic planning.

Those with the itch for real adventure realize that no one is going to give it to them. The prefabricated social life and conveyor belt career track isn't enough. If they want to embark on a daring expedition, they'll have to do it themselves. The great secret is that it's far easier than anyone imagines.

All the resources exist already within arms reach. Anything in the world you want to learn or do, anyone you want to meet, any personal challenge you want to give yourself, any skill you want to devote yourself to: *they're all doable, without anyone's permission.*

The world is waiting. It won't be found on dorm room couches. It won't be found in cinder block classrooms. It won't be given to those who simply follow the rules and don't upset the apple cart. It will be discovered–it will be created–by those daring enough to seek adventure and live life on their own terms.

The geographical territory of the earth has been largely discovered. But we're only on the borderlands of human potential. It lies before us vast, untamed, full of mystery and possibility. It will be explored by those brave enough. No special qualifications are needed beyond courage, self-honesty, a hunger for self-knowledge, and willingness to break the mold.

The great expedition of our age is the self-created journey; the self-directed life.

You're Never Done Working Hard

In *The Great Divorce*, C.S. Lewis depicts residents of hell taking a day trip to heaven. The interesting thing is that most of them don't realize they were in hell, and don't like it when they experience heaven. Most choose to go back to hell.

It's not a fire and brimstone hell, just a grey, bleak, lonely place where all the conversations and concerns are shallow. Heaven is even less like the common vision of clouds and harps. It is beautiful, but also terrifying, painful, and really, really hard. The grass and trees and water are literally hard to the touch for the visitors. Those who have been there for some time have become more substantial, and for them the blades of grass softly bend underfoot. But the visitors are such shadowy, weak, ghost-like beings that they can hardly handle the hardness of the more real heavenly environs. It takes time, effort, and struggle to be able to enjoy the wonders of this heaven. In other words, heaven isn't easy or safe, but it's good.

We often strive to find some imagined heaven—some sort of stasis where no conflict or struggle or hard work exist—and in so doing become disillusioned by the fact that we never get there. The thing is, I don't think we'd actually want it if we found it. It would look more like Lewis's hell than heaven: *safe, stagnant, dull.* A place where we become less real, and lose touch with what we want and who we are.

Think of the times when you are genuinely fulfilled, state of flow. Often they involve hard work and mental physical challenges. Even moments of apparent ease are only really enjoyable when they are earned, and when they are not indefinite, but part of a progression towards something greater still, like water stations in a marathon.

Without vision, people perish. We need goals and challenges. Not in order to get some reward or prize at the end, or to reach a state of rest, but to enjoy the challenges while we're in them. If we achieve them it's not so we can finally be done, but so that we can set our sights still higher.

Those in the story who had been in heaven for some time were working to gain more strength to scale the mountain, and then the next thing beyond it. Heaven was heaven–in full bloom and overpoweringly gorgeous–precisely because the growth never ceased. Growth only happens with work.

Don't put off enjoyment until you arrive at some imagined goal or end state. If you arrive there, it won't be that enjoyable. If you don't, you'll have missed out on the opportunity to enjoy the process itself. This doesn't mean it's just about the journey–a journey without a destination isn't a journey. It is about the destination, but because arrival means the ability to set out for the next, still greater destination as a new traveler who has grown through the trials of the previous leg.

Being fulfilled requires far more hard work than being dull, listless, or depressed. But it's worth it.

...rd Doesn't [Have to] Mean

I often write about how you can succeed by working your butt off to be the most reliable, consistent, effective person in whatever work setting you find yourself. I talk about the need to be so good and so reliable that those you work with never have to worry about you.

I once had an interesting response from a reader who said that these ideas seemed to lay the groundwork for suffering a terrible working environment. If all your focus is on working hard and making sure you don't cause stress to your colleagues, you might end up burned out and unhappy.

It's a fair criticism because I don't always make explicit an assumption that precedes the work hard advice: don't stay someplace that sucks.

Don't do things that make you dead inside. Don't stay anywhere–home, school, job, relationship–where you feel devalued or depressed every day. Don't settle or compromise. You may not know what makes you come alive, and that's OK, but as soon as you find things that make you die, quit. Exit. Leave.

Your professional life is too valuable to find some kind of middle ground or happy medium where you kind of like it OK, therefore you kind of sort of do a decent job.

No. If you're not kicking ass and being your best self day in and day out, why be there at all? If grinding it out at 100% results in your being abused or burned out, the solution is not to work less hard, it's to find new work.

If you're unhappy, slacking off a bit more will not improve the root problem. If doing your best work doesn't bring you joy, you need to find work that does.

This One Skill Will Always Win

There is one skill you can master which will guarantee everything you do will improve more over time.

The best part about this skill is it's easy. Anyone can obtain it. You don't need to have any particular natural talent. You don't need any resources or teachers to master it. Once you have it and it becomes a part of your every operation you will begin to achieve at an accelerating rate. Your success will compound and your reputation will bring you more opportunities.

In the words of Morpheus, *"Do you want to know what it is?"*

Getting shit done. That's it. Read it again. Let it sink in.

What does it look like in practice? Responding to emails immediately, and never taking longer than 24 hours to do so. Showing up for everything you've said you'd show up for. Finishing everything you've said you'd finish and on time. When you say, "I'll read that book", or, "I'll check out that website", or, "I'll send my resume", doing it. Immediately. If you can't or won't, don't say those things. Every time you say you'll do something and don't you've missed an opportunity to be better than the majority of your peers and build social capital.

In 90% of situations, I'd take someone with coherent same-day responses to all communications who always delivers as promised and when promised over someone with mastery over just about any skill I can think of. I'm not alone in this. The desperate need for hard working, reliable people who communicate immediately all the time is off the charts.

If you make people wait for responses or wonder if you'll ever follow through you've cost them, even if only psychologically. People don't tend to want to work with people who cost them. They want to work with people who they never have to expend any mental energy worrying about. They want to work with people who pleasantly surprise them by over-delivering.

Anyone can be the person who always follows through, always communicates, always delivers, and never leaves anyone hanging or in the dark. It's only a matter of will and discipline.

Just get shit done.

Be a Finisher

There are a lot of traits and skills that can make someone more valuable professionally. All of them pale in comparison to one: finishing. One can make up for a lot of deficiency in skill and experience with hard work, but not the other way around.

By 'hard work' I do not mean work that is painful or boring or time consuming. Certainly hard work can be all of these things, but if you're measuring work by how much it hurts or how long it takes, you're spinning your wheels. Hard work is work that produces something 'hard'. It creates a tangible result, and a good one. What matters is output, getting things done fast and well.

It is true, there's a trade-off between 'fast' and 'well'. While it is very important to do a job well, once it meets a certain level of quality you've got to complete it and move on. A lot of people may disagree with me, but I've observed that probably eight times out of ten, timeliness is more important than additional degrees of perfection. The key is to learn something each time about how you could have done it better, that way the quality improves with each project and the time to completion does not decrease. If you simply get things done, on time, every time without a lot of drama, and learn as you go, you will develop and excellent reputation as a highly valuable individual to work with…and herein lies the danger.

Your reputation is more important to your value in the eyes of others than is your actual product. It couldn't be any other way, as no one you work with has time to follow every detail every day of what you do. If you come through reliably, especially on some big tasks early on, you will begin to get a reputation as someone who gets things done. The longer you live up to it, the stronger the reputation becomes. At some point, you'll see diminishing returns to hard work. Your reputation will be strong enough to survive a missed project here or there. However, it's when you are most secure in your professional role that you are most vulnerable. The comfort zone is the danger zone.

The danger is not that people will suddenly realize you're no longer getting it done. That may happen, but I've witnessed people who continue to get by on a legacy of past work for years. It seems some people can spend the better part of their careers getting work because of a reputation formed decades before. The real danger is that you'll stop creating value. This is a tragedy, not only for any persons or organizations who pay you to produce, but for your own well-being. Do not underestimate the deep human need to forge and create and hone and toil and complete.

The more praise you get early on, the more you need to be alert to the temptation to slack. You've never *"arrived"*. You always need to work hard. That is what separates the good from the truly great.

The good get a well-deserved reputation and then do what's necessary to maintain it. The great put their nose to the grind 'till the end, even if their reputation would be OK if they didn't. They continue to evolve what they produce so that it is more and more what they love, but they just keep on producing.

What can you do to better your career?

How to Trump Talent Twice

One of the big secrets in the professional world is that talent is not the most valuable thing to clients, employers, coworkers, and investors. A combination of hard work and self-esteem will win out over a lot of talent, most of the time.

Hard work is the ability and willingness to do whatever it takes to get things done. Be the person who never misses a deadline, never drops the ball, never requires additional prompting, never needs to be checked-in on, never induces worry. It doesn't mean someone who just generates a lot of meaningless activity and sweat, and brags about the all-nighters or the amount of effort. The key here is the word "work". The kind of hard work that will beat talent is really hard-won results. Work needs to mean valuable outcomes, not inputs. Tangible value created.

Self-esteem is a deep connection with ones own value and meaning derived from something other than external circumstances or the approval of others. Those who can win over a room and keep it aren't the ones who crave attention or approval for their self-worth, or those who naturally have people skills, but those who don't fear looking foolish or failing because their self-esteem is much deeper than the opinion of others. They don't need to win to feel valuable, they want to win and believe they will because they already feel valuable.

These two traits are very connected. People are a lot less willing to work their butts off if their identity is wrapped up in external validation. Working hard–really hard–means being vulnerable. Being a little too cool to break a sweat shields you from potential embarrassment, but rolling up your sleeves and diving in ratchets up the risk of failing, because people may really pity you or think less if you fail when you were trying your hardest. Those with low self-esteem experience failure as catastrophic, so they rarely work at 100%.

The good news is, unlike some talents or personality traits, hard work and self-esteem can be built. You can deliberately cultivate and improve on both of them. The sooner you stop looking at external measures for your sense of worth, the easier it will be to throw yourself into something the results of which may be judged by others. The sooner you dive in to your work and resolve to consistently produce, the more you'll gain a sense of worth from your effort and the less you'll care what others say. They feed each other.

Stop worrying about how you stack up talent-wise and become unshakable in your self-esteem and unequaled in your hard work. These two things supersede all the rest, and will result in the rapid accumulation of opportunity, experience, and yes, even other highly valuable talents and skills.

Laziness Can Be Fatal

Laziness leads to boredom, and boredom is the greatest crime against oneself.

Laziness is not about physical labor. You can be bored to tears doing manual labor all day long and you can be engaged and fulfilled while lounging in a hammock.

It's hard work to live free from boredom, but it's the work of the mind and heart. It takes relentless self-discovery. You can't stay interested on a diet of quick hits of easy excitement. You need to unearth the self at the core of your being and live in accordance with what you find. You have to relentlessly purge the things that deaden your soul, bore you, and make you unhappy.

It's far easier to just go along. It's easier to do things that appear to be work but require little mental focus, discovery, or honesty.

But it's not worth the cheap sense of leisure. Living an interesting life requires the deliberate act of being interested in everything within and around you and exploring it.

Boredom is death. Laziness is terminal illness.

Break Your Once and Done Mentality

I hate to mow the lawn. Still, I love few things more than a freshly cut and edged lawn. I like the result. The problem is that only a few days later, it's already visibly growing back. It needs to be cut again. I want to be able to get it just right once and never have to deal with it again. I hate haircuts for the same reason.

I want to do things once and move on. I don't like maintenance and repeated actions. I try to carry all the grocery bags into the house in a single trip, even when it ends up taking longer and being ridiculously awkward.

I'm not going to pretend this mentality is all bad. I think it's a big strength much of the time. The main problem with it is that it creates all kinds of existential overhead. I get stressed just knowing something is in a constant state of limbo and not done for good. This stress sucks, especially when you run a business.

I've never met a business owner who loves their current website. It's always, *"Yeah, it's not what it's supposed to be. We're making some changes."* Same goes for marketing copy, sales process, product, back office, etc.

Everything is a process. You don't just build it once.

That kind of dynamism is wonderful for customers and necessary for producers, but it can be frustrating for a build-it-once-and-move-on guy like myself. I have to surround myself with people who enjoy the open-ended process yet still possess the ability and resolve to finish.

I can do it, and I do. It's necessary. But I still struggle doing it happily. It still stresses me out. I guess I can start with my lawn. If I can make my peace with the fact that grass just keeps growing back no matter how short I cut it, and embrace the rhythm and cycle, maybe I can apply that to larger things.

Skin in the Game

If you follow sports you'll notice something. Vegas is better than the experts at predicting outcomes. You could chalk this up to the wisdom of crowds, but this can't be the only explanation, because in surveys and polls the crowd doesn't do very well compared to Vegas either.

The reason Vegas is better on average than individual experts or surveyed masses is because people choose better when they have skin in the game. It's one of the reasons democracy is a bad way to determine the policies people want and grocery stores don't survey their customers to decide how to stock their shelves. When it's free, people take different and dumber risks.

Even worse than having no skin in the game is having the opposite: a cushion large enough to not only catch you if you try and fall, but one that can sustain you even if you don't try at all. Economists call this the moral hazard in the world of financial regulation. When third parties insure against risk, people and institutions make worse decisions. Think high-risk home loans underwritten by banks who knew that taxpayers would be forced to bail them out if it went south. It applies on the personal level too. While it's easy to call inheritors of wealth financially privileged, I think it's often harder to discover and live a fulfilling life if you've got a huge trust fund. If you don't have to win, it's hard to get the motivation to try.

All these examples might be too easy to agree with me on. Let's push a little farther. I think college funds cause the same problem. When parents put tens of thousands into an account that can only be used for college, young people will fall prey to the sunk cost fallacy and favor going to college much more than they would without that restricted money. Once they do, they'll take it less seriously. As long as parents are satisfied with grades and activities, it doesn't really matter. The degree is perceived as free. The opportunity cost is overlooked. The diploma at the end is supposed to guarantee a job and an income, and these are supposed to pave the way to find fulfillment. Plus, if you pick a major that is supposed to give you lots of career options, you get lulled into thinking you have infinite fallback plans. Sure, you sat in classrooms or goofed around for the first 22 years of your life, but it's all good. You've got that free degree so no matter what you do, you're set.

Parents see college as an insurance plan against all problems. They tend not to care much if you're happy there or finding your groove or learning how the world works, as long as you get a degree. Tell them you're bored and restless and opting out to go start a business or pursue a career as an artist and risk giving them a coronary. They feel more comfortable with you half-assing it through a moral hazard backed mediocrity.

Forget all that. It's your life. Whatever you do, find a way to get some skin in the game. If you don't or can't in reality, imagine and live as if you did. Find out the actual cost of your education. Tally up how much of what kind of work it would take to pay for it yourself. If it was all on you, would you pay and do it? If not, why are you doing it now? What are you willing to give up to get the things you want? If what you think you'll gain is less than what you're willing to part with, why do it?

Are you willing to fail? Are you so passionate about what you're trying to do that you've got to try it out even if it doesn't work? What if the degree fails to bring you anything you want. Will it have been worth it? If not, why do it? *"Well, I've only got another two years, so I might as well have it under my belt."* Really? Compared to what?

If you are like most people and you don't have any single passion or pursuit to throw yourself behind, no worries. Go the opposite route.

Try a bunch of stuff and build a list of things you know you don't love doing and want to avoid. Avoid them. Don't do them because they're low-risk or paid for by someone else. That's like the person who spends money they don't have on clothes they don't need because they were on sale. A $100 pair of useless jeans marked down to $50 is not a savings. It's a waste of $50. Keep eliminating things that don't bring you value and everything else is fair game.

I'm not saying it's never a good idea to take something that someone is offering to pay for. The point is to not overvalue the "free" part and undervalue the unseen costs. Not only are there often strings and expectations and the cost of forgone opportunities, often valuable things offered for free aren't even enjoyable or meaningful to you. Don't do them just because other people would call you crazy not to. And don't forget one of the biggest dangers of something someone else is paying for, which is the way it reduces your incentive to take it seriously and get the most out of it.

Look at the actions and activities in your life. Do you have skin in the game? The bigger and more important they are, the more you want to have skin in the game. It'll make you better and more likely to succeed in every way.

This is not an admonition to simply take more and bigger risks, or to alter your risk tolerance. It's an admonition to dig down deep and get to know yourself.

Discover your real risk tolerance. Be honest about what you find, whether it's more or less than you wish it were. Make decisions for you based on your unique assessment of the trade-offs involved.

Don't suffer through things because, relative to everyone else's opinion, they are low-risk or good deals or safe backup plans. Get some skin in the game. The games you want to play. On your terms.

Permission Not Necessary

A good friend told me when he was younger he would dive deep into all kinds of topics, from philosophy to physics. His dad was an intelligent guy who took some interest in these subjects, but also a practical man focused on results. He was a businessman and a pastor, and looked for direct application of ideas.

My friend had a book on quantum mechanics sitting in the house, and his dad asked him what it was all about. A minute or two in to giving a breakdown, his dad said, "That sounds really interesting", then moved on to whatever he was doing next. My friend assumed his dad was just humoring him. The next Sunday during the sermon his dad worked in some profound points relating concepts of quantum mechanics to the topic at hand. My friend was amused, impressed, and also a little frustrated.

How could his dad hear two minutes on the concept and then start using it to illustrate a point? My friend had read dozens of books on it and still did not feel the permission to write or speak on it with laypeople, or attempt to draw life lessons.

What my friend failed to realize at the time is that he didn't need anyone's permission to use ideas. You can dive into new concepts and start playing with them and putting them to use the way a kid might if he discovered a new type of Lego block. It's true, you may misunderstand or misuse them, but isn't that what you did when you first jumped on a bike or first picked up a baseball bat?

Sometimes, people are so passionate about truth and understanding that they become slaves to expertise and fear any effort to describe or utilize ideas. What if they're wrong? It's prudent to desire a firm grasp of something before you start spouting off, but there is a real danger in believing you can't act until your understanding is complete.

It's a paradoxical kind of arrogance to keep your nose in books until you've mastered every angle of an idea, because it assumes that you can master every angle of an idea. You can't. It doesn't mean you shouldn't try, but it does mean you can give yourself permission to play with ideas, discuss them, test them, implement them even while you're exploring them.

Yes, if you read the book instead of watching the movie version, or worse yet the preview alone, you will understand the story better. Still, a great many stories can be understood enough to be useful based on just the trailer.

As long as you believe only experts can engage certain ideas you will operate with an extremely limited paradigm.

Go ahead, tackle a new topic and see how you can use it right away. Sometimes the novice understanding opens up new avenues the experts are blind to.

The Power of Perception

Our disposition toward reality is often more important to our happiness than reality.

Consider the following differences in perception.

Before vacuuming the inside of my car:
"This thing is a beater. It takes too long to start, it sounds loud, I think it's misfiring, the transmission is near shot and it has no pickup left. I just hope it lasts me another few weeks."

After vacuuming the inside of the my car:
"This thing has a lot of pep! It rides so smooth for its age, and it really has some zip. I bet this car can last another ten years!"

Even if perception does not alter physical reality, it alters emotional and psychological reality and our emotional and psychological experience is what determines our happiness in the moment.

For instance, what kind of car I drive doesn't determine our happiness. How we feel about the car we have does. What kind of misfortune befalls us does not dictate our happiness, but how we interpret and process that misfortune and the narrative we build around it.

I have a friend I consider to be a master at creating a fun narrative and living in accordance with it. For instance, when he comes home and his power is shut off due to an unpaid bill, he laughs and chalks it up to the story of his unpredictable and fun-filled life. He actually gets more jokes and stories out of the ordeal, so it's a plus. I remember he was elated when an overdue parking ticket resulted in him being pulled over and going to jail. When he energetically tells the story, it actually makes you jealous it didn't happen to you. But if it actually did happen to me I would've been pissed. It would have ruined my day. It didn't ruin his.

Circumstances don't change in any objective sense due to our feelings about them (though the way we approach them can lead to different outcomes). But the level of enjoyment or stress in those circumstances does.

Back to my car. It will last as long as it lasts. Physical realities, not my feelings, will determine when the engine finally conks out. Besides doing basic maintenance, I can't change or control that. It will happen when it happens. But I can alter my quality of life in whatever number of days I left driving my car. I can experience those as enjoyable days or stressful days. If I vacuum my car out, it makes it feel less old and increases the enjoyment level and decreases the stress.

That small act alters my perception of the situation and increases my quality of life. It matters.

As Long as It's Interesting, It's Good

Many young people think they know what industry or category of job they want. They're mostly wrong.

We're trained by the school and university process to think in terms of big career categories and majors. *Marketing. Hospitality. Management. Financial Services.* But these categories are so generic and ill defined that they offer almost no value for an individual trying to forge a path to life and career success.

The truth is, you have no idea what industry or job will make you happy. How could you? You've barely seen any of them up close. The roles within these industry labels can be more diverse than you can imagine. Many jobs and entire industries have no label. Many more will emerge that don't yet exist.

The good news is that this is good news. Opportunity abounds and what major you pick or what label you spit out when someone asks what you want to do are of little importance. You have massive flexibility and a chance to explore and experiment. You can even create new roles that no one ever thought of.

Stop stressing about it. Don't fret over getting an internship that perfectly aligns with your imagined industry of choice. As long as you're not doing something you hate, you're heading in the right direction. You don't know what you'll discover.

You can't learn it from a course catalog or guidance counselor. You've got to engage the world and see what you respond to and what responds to you.

Not only that, but it is well documented that 'outsiders' are most likely to innovate. If you go directly from a finance major to an investment banking internship and then job, you'll have experiences and knowledge identical to nearly everyone you work with.

If you first spend a few years working at a software startup, building a network of owners of financial service businesses, then transition into investment banking, you'll have a perspective and paradigm that makes you truly unique. You'll have a network that most of your peers lack. You'll be able to do that thing which is the holy grail of the creative process, and create a new intersection of separate matrices of thought.

Your theories about what industry or job fits you are like all theories. They need to be tested. Go try some stuff. Anything you don't dislike is fair game. You might discover new roles you never thought of. You might invent a new industry or join it as it emerges. You might gain a distinct advantage and a unique outlook, network, and experience set by working somewhere unlikely first.

Don't try to pick your industry yet. In fact, don't ever pick one. Just do interesting stuff. Don't worry about the rest.

Conclusion: Take Back Your Joy

Many people live with undesirable circumstances. Perhaps they're working an unenjoyable job, wasting away inside a classroom, or feeling trapped in a failing relationship. The details don't matter much. Whatever the case may be, in every undesirable circumstance there is a way out.

Occasionally, the only escape might be a change of disposition toward the situation. An attitude adjustment, if you will. But more often than not, real, tangible avenues to a better life exist all around if only we are willing to look.

Sometimes, admitting the truth might be the most difficult step. We are, many of us, governed by an immutable pride that works as much in our favor as it does against us. To declare our present state of affairs is less than ideal might feel like an admission of weakness or an error on our part. But if we are honest with ourselves, little calculation is ever required to determine whether we're in a place we want to be or not. We'll usually know right away.

Once you do muster the courage to confess your dissatisfaction, you must act immediately with your resolve fully intact. If you do not, you risk more than losing your conviction. You also set yourself up to become a cynic– chronically afflicted, yet committed to suffering. Like a smoker diagnosed with early-stage cancer who refuses to stop. In refusing to act, you choose to remain enslaved to your situation, and, whatever sympathy you might once have had will evaporate.

No one else will make the decision to escape for you. Not your parents. Not your spouse. Not your friends. Not your boss. No one else. Only you can change the hand you've been dealt. It might sound disempowering. On the contrary, the same principle grants you more power than you might be aware. Just as no one will make the choice for you, no one can stop you either. If you're unhappy and choose to make a change, the most important person to be on board is you. Everyone else that matters will come around to the new you sooner or later.

You might find yourself in a situation so toxic that it warrants no explanation. An abrupt jailbreak is the only logical course of action. In such a case escaping what you hate right away might be more important than your presentation or delivery.

On other occasions, thoughtful analysis might be more appropriate. Maybe even seeking guidance from a friend will be in order. The procedures are not important. What is important is that you are fully committed to the decision you make once you make it, no matter how you arrive there. Moving forward in a state of limbo or uncertainty will make the transition more difficult, and potentially lead to an even greater state of dissatisfaction than before.

I've been told on the brink of my escape that my flight mechanism was stronger than my fight. Only cowards run away from their problems. The first time I heard this it infuriated me, and my pride was insulted. It continued to bother me until I came to terms with the real issue at hand. People who are not actively working to improve their own circumstances will attempt to stifle the efforts of others around them.

There's nothing weak about changing your mind or abandoning ideas that no longer serve you. In fact, I believe it's a sign of great strength, no matter how incomprehensible it may seem to others around you. You do not have to remain where you are. You owe no one an explanation if you don't choose to provide one. Selfishly fight for your happiness, and don't let anyone discourage you.

Once you've made the leap, the real work begins.

Escaping what you hate is the easy part. Creating a life you love can be incredibly difficult. Once unburdened the whole world is at your doorstep. What will you choose? Where will you go? What will you do?

Don't fret. You don't have to figure it out. Distance yourself from the things you hate you just escaped. Write them off your list of possibilities and proceed boldly ahead, open to what may come. Maintain an acute awareness of new ideas, people, experiences, and places that you don't enjoy as you identify them, and adapt accordingly.

It is in this process of continually identifying and eliminating activities you don't enjoy, that you will narrow the field of play for yourself. Consider it your own personal refining process, sorting the wheat from the chaff, and discovering what makes you come alive.

When you find something that brings you joy, pursue it. If it begins to bring you dread, move on. Lather. Rinse. Repeat.

The purpose of this philosophy, *Don't Do Stuff You Hate*, is not to develop a non-committal attitude toward life. In fact, quite the opposite. It is to cultivate your highest potential by pursuing activities that yield the most fulfillment and satisfaction for you.

Whether you find this in a new job, in new friends, in a new city, or a new hobby is up to you, your preferences, and your own unique experience. Do not settle for a meaningless, unfulfilling existence. You are meant for more.

About the Authors

Isaac Morehouse is the Founder and CEO of Praxis, a professional boot camp and startup apprenticeship program for those who want more than college. He is the author of six books and hosts a weekly podcast on education, entrepreneurship, and big ideas. Isaac is dedicated to the relentless pursuit of freedom, for himself and others. He blogs regularly at isaacmorehouse.com.

Mitchell Earl is a writer, photographer, and business development professional passionate about advancing individual and economic liberty through entrepreneurship. He's an Oklahoma native, a middle brother of five siblings, and uncle of a beautiful niece and an ornery, handsome nephew.

He has an extensive background building organizations that includes co-founding a campus brand of a national media company, launching his own freelance business, serving as an executive for multiple youth organizations, working for a former Bar Association president, facilitating youth seminars for a non-profit think tank, and apprenticing for the Founder/CEO of a venture-funded startup.

Today, when he's not busy empowering entrepreneurs or brainstorming business ideas, he can be found reading, writing, shooting hoops, walking his Bernese Mountain Dog, playing poker and smoking cigars with his friends, or expanding his craft beer palette in Charleston, South Carolina, where he lives.

Made in the USA
Middletown, DE
24 February 2021